Country Roads

~ of ~

ILLINOIS

A Country Roads
Guide Book

Country Roads
~ of ~
ILLINOIS

Marcia Schnedler

Illustrated by
Victoria Sheridan

Country Roads of Illinois

Published by Country Roads Press
P.O. Box 286, Lower Main Street
Castine, Maine 04421

Text and cover design by Edith Allard.
Lyrics from "The Illinois & Michigan Canal," page 39, by
   Kevin O'Donnell/Arranmore Music © ℗ 1986.
Library of Congress Catalog Card No. 92-073120
ISBN 1-56626-003-5

Printed in the United States of America.
10 9 8 7 6 5 4 3 2 1

Library of Congress Cataloging-in-Publication Data

Schnedler, Marcia
       Country roads of Illinois / Marcia Schnedler ;
illustrated by Victoria Sheridan.
              p.   cm.
       Includes index.
       ISBN 1-56626-003-5 (pbk.) : $9.95
       1. Illinois--Tours.   2. Automobile travel--Illinois--
Guidebooks.
       I. Title.
       F539.3.S34   1992   92-73120
       917.7304'43--dc20   CIP

To my parents, Richard and Harriet Chambers,
born and bred in Illinois

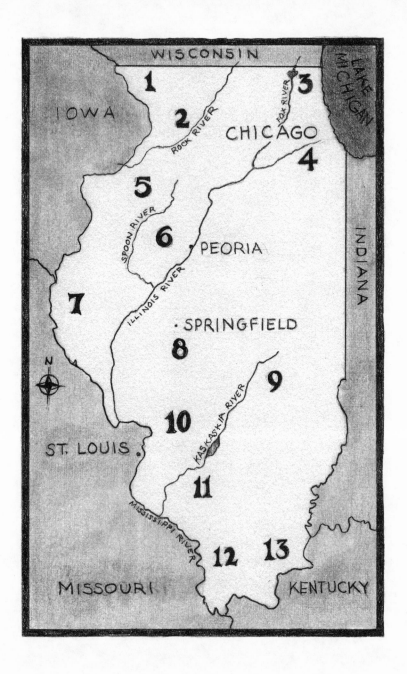

Contents

(& Key to Illinois Country Roads)

Introduction

My roots are in Illinois. My great-great-great-grandfather arrived in the state in May 1844, bringing his family from northern Pennsylvania in a pair of canvas-covered lumber wagons called prairie schooners. My parents were born and raised in the state, and I've lived in Chicago most of my adult life.

So I was delighted at the opportunity to travel the country roads of my home state. Like many of us, I had neglected to explore my own backyard, opting instead to visit more "exotic" spots. Touring the state's small towns and rural byways rekindled childhood memories of Thanksgiving spreads at my grandmother's home in Seward, a farm town of 100 people west of Rockford. I vividly recall walking the block from her house to the general store and post office, where I was barely tall enough to see the top of the wood counter. I remember hiking several miles from Seward to my aunt and uncle's dairy farm, where I admired my three cousins performing their daily chores.

Along with my own memories, I rediscovered historical figures from my schoolbooks, such as Father Pierre Marquette and Louis Jolliet on their 1673 exploratory voyage from Lake Michigan to the Illinois River. I tried to imagine their first view of the cliffs at Starved Rock, or their excitement at reaching the broad Mississippi River that would take them south.

I met Abraham Lincoln again, and became more fascinated than ever with this quintessential self-made man and most human of national heroes.

On this book's baker's dozen of routes through Illinois,

you'll meet them, too, while discovering captivating corners like the Amish country south of Champaign-Urbana; Kewanee, the Hog Capital of the World; Galesburg, a railroad crossroads that inspired the poetry of Carl Sandburg; the Illinois & Michigan Canal, a narrow channel that changed the upper Midwest forever; and funky Mississippi River towns.

We'll follow routes through the northernmost regions of Illinois, where flatlands dissolve into low, close-packed hills dotted with dairy farms and historic hamlets. And we'll travel through the state's very different southern tip, marked by forested Ozark hills of convoluted limestone that give way to cypress and tupelo swamps reminiscent of Louisiana bayous.

You'll find plenty of offbeat and amusing sights: a French restaurant in a bowling alley; a luxurious bed and breakfast in a furniture store; a two-story outhouse known as the "skyscrapper"; the grave of a circus elephant killed by lightning; the tomb of a World War II hero pig. You may grieve as I did at the shuttered small-town storefronts and abandoned barns and farmhouses left behind in this bigger-is-better era . . . while just down the road, you may pause to admire a Victorian home as spruced up as when its first owner moved in a hundred years ago.

Communities are expressing more pride in their heritage than ever, opening small museums and restoring historic buildings at a great rate. Such sites reflect the midwestern love of place, and provide numerous interesting stops for country-road wanderers. (Many such museums and sites are open seasonally or only on certain days of the week, so I suggest you call ahead to those you especially want to see.)

Excellent resources available through regional and local tourist offices can supplement what you find in this book. and sites are open seasonally or only on certain days of the week, so I suggest you call ahead to those you especially want to see.)

Excellent resources available through regional and local tourist offices can supplement what you find in this book. Among their brochures are listings of special events. Browsing through them, you'll realize that Illinoisans love a good time: they put on thousands of festivals each year. Some celebrate their farm heritage with events devoted to threshing, quilting, and other skills; or to sweet corn, pork chops, or Holsteins. Raggedy Ann, Popeye, Superman, and Dick Tracy are honored in their Illinois "hometowns." Encampments at sites of the French and Indian War, Revolutionary War, Black Hawk War, and Civil War create exciting living history.

And if that's not enough, keep your eyes peeled for homemade signs advertising pancake dinners and bingo nights. Check out bulletins posted in cafés or drugstore windows that can lead you to a church bake sale or PTA craft fair. At these events—and just about everywhere along Illinois country roads—you can count on small-town hospitality.

Our routes lead you to many of the Prairie State's most attractive parks and natural areas. The Illinois Department of Conservation produces brochures that put you onto everything from fine state-owned lodges and camping sites to bicycle, hiking, and horseback trails, canoe waterways and winter sports spots. Also take advantage of a host of preserves and parks operated by counties and towns, as well as natural areas protected by organizations such as The Nature Conservancy.

You can call the State of Illinois tourism office at 800-223-0121 for general visitor information. You can call the Illinois Department of Conservation 217-782-7454. The state Department of Agriculture has a guide to direct sale fruit and vegetable markets, which you can get through the Illinois tourism office or by writing to Illinois Department of Agriculture, Division of Marketing, State Fairgrounds, P.O. Box 19281, Springfield, IL 62794-9281. Regional and local tourism offices and chambers of commerce, listed at the end of each chapter, also can be of great assistance.

One final thing you'll discover along these routes is that your travel dollars take you a lot further once you leave the big cities and their suburbs behind—all the more reason to explore the appealing *Country Roads of Illinois.*

1 ~

Northwest Passage

Take I-90, the Northwest Tollway, from Chicago to Rockford (about 86 miles), skirt around Rockford on US 20, and continue west on US 20 to Freeport, about 120 miles from Chicago. The first part of the trip runs from Freeport to Galena. Then we head south from Galena along the Mississippi River and inland to Mount Carroll. For maximum enjoyment, this trip requires two or three days.

Highlights: *Freeport, Steam Threshing Show and Antique Display, Galena, Land O' Corn Café, cheese companies, Apple River Canyon State Park; stagecoach, covered-wagon, and hayrides; Bishop's Busy Big Store; llama, Christmas tree, and mallard duck farms; Mississippi Palisades State Park, Timber Lake Playhouse, antiques, arts, and crafts.*

Galena, in the extreme northwest corner of Illinois, was a rough-and-tumble lead-mining boomtown in 1830. By the 1850s, its accumulated wealth dazzled in a display of American architecture arrayed up steep, terraced hillsides cut by the Galena River. But the mines petered out, the river silted up, and Galena's prosperity faded, revived only in recent decades by big-city folks fixing up getaway homes. Then tourists began to arrive by the bus load.

Most travelers hurry straight to Galena, catching only quick glimpses along the way of wide views over rugged hills never softened or flattened by the Ice Age glaciers that covered most of Illinois. We'll explore two routes through the striking and equally historic surrounding countryside. The first travels the stagecoach trail of the mid-1800s from Freeport to Galena. The second heads south from Galena along the Mississippi River. You'll find antiques, arts, and crafts everywhere.

The Stagecoach Trail

"Go, Pretzels!"

That's the cry of Freeport High School, whose twisted, salted mascot honors the German-Americans returning east from the Galena mines who got this far and decided to stay. My great-grandmother Anne McCaleb Sheets wrote of her own move there in 1920, "I loved the old German town with its Meierkorts and Billerbecks, its Machamers and Kautenburgs, its Poffenbergers and Pieffenthalers; its Spotless Town housewives and its old cookie recipes; its 'made the door open,' and 'outen the lights,' Of course, since we were there during Prohibition days, we didn't know it in its best days, when there were almost a hundred saloons for the 23,000 inhabitants; but as they were the decent, German type of saloon, I'm almost sorry I didn't meet a few of them."

Freeport's beginnings were equally colorful. The land-locked community received its maritime name because of William "Tutty" Baker, who settled here in 1835 and operated a ferry across the Pecatonica River. The generous Tutty offered free rides, meals, and lodging to many travelers. His hardworking wife quipped that since the place was such a free port for passersby, he might as well call his new town by that name. Tutty Baker Days each August, the county's largest festival, honors him with music, historical tours, carriage rides, a beer garden, and other activities.

Today Freeport straddles the main east–west route to Galena just as it did in the 1830s when it was a stop on the Frink & Walker stage line from Chicago. Now it's an agricultural hub serving much of Stephenson and Jo Daviess counties, the top dairy producers of Illinois where almost 50,000 cattle—largely black-and-white Holsteins—troop into their stalls twice a day, seven days a week, for milking.

Each June, Freeporters salute their economic butter (and bread) at an Ag Breakfast where you can enjoy bountiful farm-cooked food, a 4-H petting zoo, entertainment, and tours. The breakfast is held at a different farm each year, and starts at 6:00 A.M.—when any dairy farmer has already been up awhile—and runs through the morning.

In July, hundreds of gas engines and tractors chug away at Freeport's twenty-five-year-old Steam Threshing Show and Antique Display. City folks can get the hang of the old-fashioned aerobic exercise involved in threshing, shredding, corn shelling, and baling. Country crafts are demonstrated and the place is packed with antiques. During the show and on other dates from May through October, a thirty-six-ton 1912 Heisler gear-driven steam locomotive pulls a passenger flatcar and a 101-year-old wooden caboose along a four-mile ride through farm fields and forests.

Leave Freeport on US 20 west. As the road rolls across farm fields, keep your eye peeled for turn-of-the-century barns with the date of construction painted proudly over the doors. Turn north (right) into Lena.

"Leapin' Lena," as it likes to be known, was a stop on the Chicago–Galena stagecoach route. Samuel F. Dodds built an inn (now a private home) in 1848 on Lena Street as a way station on the five-day or longer journey. Later the railroad sliced through Lena, and grain and seed elevators now huddle between the tracks and Main Street.

Along Main Street, Kayser's Butchering is worth a stop if only for the savory smell. Willie Kayser came from Germany and began his career as a butcher who made house calls: farmers would ask him to stop by to kill and dress chickens.

Now he has won state and national awards for his hams, bacon, dried beef, and sausages. The mouth-watering aroma of smoked meats will transport you to Willie's Old World.

Down the street, the Land O' Corn Café, named for an Illinois Central passenger train that used to stop in Lena, may be the ultimate farm-town eatery as well as the social center for overall-clad farmers in town to do business at the supply stores. I filled up on thick cream of broccoli soup worthy of a four-star gourmet spot (real cream is the secret) and a tasty tuna salad sandwich, all for a trifling $2.25.

Surrounded by all that milk and cream, it's no surprise that Lena and neighboring towns are the site of award-winning cheese companies. Cheese-lovers should detour back to U.S. 20, then west four or five miles to Kolb-Lena Cheese. The late food critic James Beard pronounced its Brie and Camembert the finest produced in America. Other varieties such as smoked Swiss are mighty fine, too. North of Lena, at Route 73 and Louisa Road, Torkelson Cheese Company creates award-winning Muenster.

Once you've cheesed it in Lena, head northwest out of town on Lena Street, which becomes the North Stagecoach Trail. Tracks of the railroad that put the coach line out of business run more or less parallel all the way to Galena. The surrounding hills were the site of fighting during the 1832 Black Hawk War, which drove Native Americans from their beloved lands and opened northern Illinois to settlers. You'll pass a pioneer cemetery, all that's left of an 1837 settlement near Waddams Hill, where the county's first permanent resident broke the sod. Beware of slow-moving tractors on the road, especially when you come over the top of a hill. Passing drivers often give you a friendly wave.

In Warren, a feed-store silo blends into the small, turn-of-the-century downtown. The village's sturdy Federal-style stone community building was originally the Tisdel Hotel, built in 1851 to put up stagecoach passengers. If you happen to be in town on the right June weekend, you'll find that automobiles have been evicted from more than fifty garages to stage Warren's all-town garage sale and flea market.

If you arrive in Warren before 10:30 A.M., you can watch workers "cut the curd" and "put the stretch" in mozzarella at the Warren Cheese Plant on the west edge of town. Their specialty is Apple Jack, created by owner John Bussman from cultures of Monterey Jack, cheddar, and Swiss.

Stockton lies south of Warren on Route 78 at U.S. 20, and makes a pleasant detour. Once its prosperous lead smelters ran full blast, but when the mines closed, Stockton became an agricultural center.

In the days of flower children, midwestern folk musicians began gathering the last weekend of August at the white, wooden Willow Methodist Church south of Stockton on Willow Road. They still come, performing from a haywagon out in front of the church. Former hippies bring their children and grandchildren to the concerts. Yuppies and local farmers come, too. The musicians camp in a cow pasture across from the church and jam into the night.

Leave Warren on Galena Avenue, which becomes Stagecoach Trail again and crosses gentle hills dappled with dairy farms. Turn south (left) on North Canyon Park Road to Apple River Canyon State Park. Geologists love this park because it's part of an unglaciated region called the Driftless Area. For botanists, it's the only spot in Illinois where certain plants such as birdseye primrose, American stickseed, moschatel, jeweled shooting star, purple melic grass, and other rare species grow.

Historians ponder the nefarious Daves brothers who originally settled here and named their section of the Apple River "Hell's Branch." Later pioneers cleaned up the place and changed the name to Millville, but what was left of the town by the late 1800s washed away when a dam broke upstream. For the rest of us, the park is simply an idyllic spot where the river cuts a fan of sheer-walled cliffs through the limestone. Walkers will enjoy the trails that wind along the canyons and cliffs.

Take the Stagecoach Trail through the hamlet of Apple River. Just past town is Stagecoach Trails Livery, where you'll find a replica of an 1848 Concord coach. "I always enjoyed the big, heavy horses and always wanted a stagecoach," said the crusty owner, R.J. Spillane. "But I found out how much they cost, so I built one." Spillane raises one-ton Belgian workhorses that haul groups of eight to ten visitors on stagecoach rides along some of the old trails, on hayrides, or on covered-wagon drives. He likes passengers to ride shotgun, as in the old days, and help drive. Call ahead for reservations.

Continue west. Scales Mound, north of the road and across the train tracks, is a village of old white frame homes and mostly shuttered commercial buildings. The day I passed through, the main excitement was provided by workers digging a hole in front of the Sinclair station; thirteen sidewalk superintendents were watching. Charles Mound, the highest point in Illinois at 1,235 feet, rises a bit northeast of town and is simply a large, gently sloping hill covered in corn.

The Stagecoach Trail winds through more and more closely packed hills, and rides a ridge for a while, with farms in the valleys and gullies below before emerging in Galena.

Alternate Route to Galena. Intrepid motorists happy to forge cross-country south from Scales Mound to Elizabeth will be rewarded with some of the finest vistas in Illinois. A copy of the Galena/Jo Daviess County Recreation Guide and Map will help you find your way.

At Scales Mound, go south from the Stagecoach Trail on Elizabeth Scales Mound Road—through steep hills dissected by narrow, winding creeks. Occasional outcrops of sedimentary rock look as though they're made of fossilized pastry flakes. Ridges, mounds, and valleys are covered in a patterned quilt of fields and forest dotted with white barns and farmhouses.

Follow signs toward tiny Schapville, where on an ordinary day the loudest noises are the calls of cardinals and crickets. In mid-July, Shepherd of the Hills Lutheran Church has an ice cream social and bazaar with delectable pies, cakes, and quilts. Neighboring Zion Presbyterian Church holds an early-August supper, bazaar, and folk/gospel concert highlighting pressed chicken sandwiches, pies galore, and local talent. Take gravel-covered Stadel Road at the Presbyterian Church, jogging left across Menzemer to Grube Road, which runs back into paved Elizabeth Scales Mound Road, which in turn leads to Elizabeth.

Elizabeth lies on busy US 20. Stop downtown at 100-year-old Bishop's Busy Big Store, the quintessential country store advertising fresh chicken (just in), bulk pickled herring, and creamery butter. Inside, you'll find an old-fashioned tin ceiling and an oak-and-mirrors meat cooler. The store is crammed with everything from "overhauls" in sizes "aught" (0) to 50, to salted-in-the-shell peanuts. Once silent movies and vaudeville shows entertained customers on the second floor.

Next door, David Seagraves creates wood and stone sculptures and carvings, largely on commission, and will give you a look. He was working on an intricate crucifix and angels for a church in a Chicago suburb the day I stopped in. Afterward, take US 20 west to Galena.

Popular Galena is the subject of guidebooks all on its own, as are the forty or more inns and bed and breakfasts throughout the area. Galena ranks as one of the finest antiquing towns in the Midwest. In addition, an antiques auction occurs virtually every weekend from April through October; look in the local *Galena Gazette* for place and time. Bidding often gets stiff, but at least prices are wholesale rather than retail.

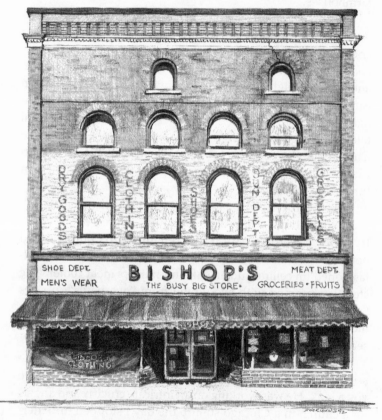

Bishop's Busy Big Store in Elizabeth,
the quintessential country store

Check what's going on at Galena's Turner Hall. There's bingo every Thursday at 7 P.M. and the hall is also the scene of concerts six times a year by the Galena Chamber Ensemble comprised of Chicago Symphony Orchestra members and guests. One Saturday each month, March through October, a local bluegrass group hosts the Plum River Country Opera.

Jakels' Galena Bäckerie & Café, operated by Gunther and Astrid Jakel, draws customers from miles around with mouth-watering European breads and pastries such as caraway rye, linzertorte, and black-and-white Holstein-cow cookies. You can sample the wares here for breakfast or lunch. When you're stuffed and rested, head into the next part of our trip.

Galena to Mount Carroll

As the Galena River flows, it's only a few miles from town to the Mississippi River. In Galena's heyday, this wealthy mining community was also a major port on the Upper Mississippi. The Galena River long ago silted up, but the Mississippi remains a busy artery. This part of our trip travels south from Galena along the mighty river, through the hills and bluffs lining its shores.

Just east of the Galena River on US 20, turn south on Blackjack Road off 4th Street. Within blocks, you're into the countryside on a winding, hilly blacktop road. You'll find few of the artfully restored nineteenth-century residences along here that you saw back in Galena—just working farms and mobile homes. If you're out early, you may spot some wild turkeys crossing a hillside field on a foggy morning.

You can walk with a llama through the meadows and wooded hills of Green Valley Farm, managed by Terry and Ginny Carroll. Reach it by turning left off Blackjack Road onto Irish Hollow Road. The farm, named for the 1913 country school that stands on the property, raises the South American beasts of burden along with fallow deer. You can go on two-hour hikes with the graceful llamas on trails across the farm's 250 acres. Call ahead for information.

Back on Blackjack Road, Och's Christmas Tree Farm, open Thanksgiving through Christmas, grows Scotch pine, Norway spruce, white and red pine, Douglas fir, Austrian pine, blue and white spruce, and balsam fir. If your fingers are freezing after you stalk and saw the perfect tree, the warming house serves hot beverages. It's a full-service Christmas stop: wreaths, swags of evergreen branches, stands, and ornaments are also for sale.

As you continue south on Blackjack Road, you'll notice a heap of tailings left from the old mines. If it has rained recently, gray slime will have washed across the road. Along this section, the ride becomes a gentle roller coaster, and at one point, you'll travel a fifteen percent incline—about as steep as it gets in Illinois.

Follow the signs to Chestnut Mountain Resort, busiest when its sixteen ski runs are open (Thanksgiving through St. Patrick's Day). This isn't quite the Rockies: there's a 475-foot vertical drop, and the longest run is 3,500 feet. In summer you can have lunch, ascend the chairlift for panoramic views over the Mississippi and its bluffs, and hike well kept trails through the woods.

Continue winding along Blackjack Road into Hanover, which declares itself the World's Mallard Duck Capital. It almost certainly is, thanks to Whistling Wings, Inc., operated by the Whalen family. Some 200,000 mallards are hatched here each year and shipped to hunting preserves, conservation groups, research scientists, and other customers—who have included Japan's late Emperor Hirohito. Offices and hatchery are at 113 Washington Street.

Visitors to Whistling Wings can view six-foot-tall incubators that hold up to 15,000 eggs, with hatchings programmed to meet orders and shipping schedules. (You can also purchase smoked and frozen mallard, dressed pheasant, wild turkey, partridge, and quail.) Some hatchlings are shipped to customers wanting day-old ducks. The rest are moved to confinement buildings at the Whistling Wings farm south of town on Route 84. When five weeks old, the ducklings are introduced to life's harsh realities in a wetland area where they grow up just like wild ducks, predators and all. When they're full grown and it's shipping time, food is used to coax them into the catching areas.

Breeder ducks are kept at the farm, too, in four pens holding 1,000 hens and 400 drakes each. The farm isn't open to the public, but you can't miss it from the highway.

Hanover holds a Mallardfest each September, when visitors can adopt a duck, name it, and release it into the wild. They can also dine on duckwurst and sloppy ducks, or buy duck souvenirs ranging from T-shirts to fertilizer.

Alternate Route to Hanover. Here's an off-the-beaten-path route for adventuresome motorists. Shortly after leaving Galena on Blackjack Road, turn west (right) on Pilot Knob Road. It becomes River Road and hugs the Mississippi. This gravel road, filled with more than its share of potholes, takes you through some exquisite landscape, but be warned that in winter and after rainstorms it is sometimes impassable. It's also unsuitable for recreational vehicles, vans, and drivers who worry about blemishing their cars' paint.

If you go, you'll spot picturesque farmhouses and barns tucked at the base of bluffs with bottomland fields fanning out before them. An occasional junkyard, tavern, and clump of riverside cottages are scattered among the scenic beauty. Inside Blanding Landing Recreation Area, a park and boat landing near a lock and dam, a sign warns that the "Road Ends in Water 100 Feet." Locals must have bailed out a few overenthusiastic drivers. From Blanding, cut inland and up the bluffs to Hanover.

After you've explored Hanover, head south on Route 84. At first, the road tracks along the Apple River as it squiggles toward the Mississippi. High fences surround the Savanna Army Depot just the other side of busy freight-train tracks. As you reach Mississippi Palisades State Park, you finally sight the river. Turn right into the park's boat ramp area for a closer look. In warm weather, a barge may be shoving its way north carrying coal or charging south filled with grain. In winter, keep an eye out for ducks diving for morsels and bald eagles swooping for fish. If the river is frozen thickly enough, well-insulated fishermen may be hauling in their catch through holes chopped in the ice.

Inside the park, paved roads lead to views across the expanse of river, wooded islands, and bottomlands. The palisades, a line of lofty cliffs and deep ravines eroded into intriguing shapes, comprise its most dramatic element. If you're lucky, a striking pileated woodpecker will be drilling a hole in a tree or wild turkeys will be pecking for insects in a field. You might glimpse a mink, a fox, or a deer, too—or at least their tracks.

The river town of Savanna lies about three miles south of the palisades. There you'll find a good-sized marina with campsites located practically downtown, and riverbank markets selling bait, catfish, and smoked fish. The Pulford Opera House on Main Street has been restored into a chock-full antique mall where you could spend *hours*. But if that's not enough, try the Eatery Antiques café and shop four doors down.

Head east on US 52/Route 64 to Mount Carroll, a well-off nineteenth-century farming community proud of its numerous historic homes. Like many Illinois communities, the town got its start with a grain mill. Mount Carroll received its first shot in the arm when it became a county seat in 1843, and a second in 1853 when a seminary opened its doors there.

The seminary grew into four-year Shimer College, which unfortunately closed its doors in 1978. The handsome campus, largely built early in this century, is now the Campbell Center for Historic Preservation Studies, with workshops and courses on preserving everything from masonry to antique fabrics. Mount Carroll's small downtown surrounds the county courthouse, which is graced by a Civil War monument topped with Lorado Taft's cavalryman sculpture.

Timber Lake Playhouse, the oldest semiprofessional summer stock theater in Illinois, draws an audience from throughout the region—which undoubtedly helps fill a number of bed and breakfasts in town and on nearby farms. (At one called The Farm, you can nest in a former chicken coop, complete with TV, fireplace, stone terrace, and refrigerator. Its main building is a 125-year-old farmhouse.)

The Playhouse brings in young talent from across the country. It is located south of town, to the east of Route 78. The handsome wood building is set among tall trees next to a campground and a man-made lake. From here, signs lead you from Timber Lake Road to Oakville Country School Museum, a red brick one-room schoolhouse, log cabin, and blacksmith shop tucked between an old cemetery and a golf course—a peaceful country setting for the end of our trip.

If you're heading north or east from here, keep your eye out for oval-shaped corn cribs with cupolas on top. This particular design for the practical storage units was all the rage among trendy area farmers seventy or so years ago.

In the Area

Northern Illinois Tourism Council, 150 N. Ninth Street, Rockford, IL 61107: 815-964-6482 or 800-248-6482

Stephenson County Convention and Visitors Bureau (Freeport): 800-369-2955

Galena/Jo Daviess County Convention and Visitors Bureau (Galena): 815-777-3557 or 800-747-9377

Mount Carroll Chamber of Commerce: 815-244-9161

Stephenson County Historical Society Museum (Freeport): 815-232-8419

Apple River Canyon State Park (Apple River): 815-745-3302

Stagecoach Trail Livery (Apple River): 815-594-2423

Green Valley Farm (Galena): 815-777-2183

Och's Christmas Tree Farm (Galena): 319-588-0897 (main number)

Chestnut Mountain Resort (Galena): 800-397-1320

Whistling Wings, Inc. (Hanover): 815-591-2206

Mississippi Palisades State Park (Savanna): 815-273-2731

The Farm Bed and Breakfast (Mount Carroll): 815-244-9885

Timber Lake Playhouse (Mount Carroll): 815-244-2035

2 ~

Rock River Valley

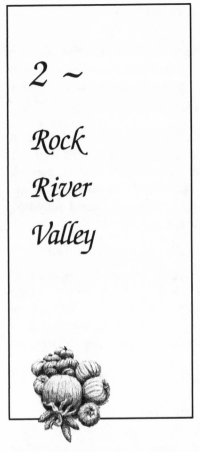

From Chicago: Take I-90, the Northwest Tollway, to Rockford (about 86 miles), skirt around Rockford on US 20, and turn off on Route 2, which follows the Rock River.

From Dubuque, Iowa: Take US 20 east to Rockford, then go south on Route 2. This trip runs from Rockford to Dixon along the river.

Highlights: *Limestone bluffs along the river; Castle Rock State Park; John Deere Historic Site; Jarrett Prairie Center, Lowden State Park, White Pines State Park; Oregon's Autumn on Parade festival; Ronald Reagan's boyhood home.*

"Rock River was a beautiful country," said Black Hawk, the Sauk chief, after losing his northern Illinois land to the white settlers. "I loved my towns, my cornfields, and the home of my people. I fought for it. It is now yours. Keep it, as we did."

Our route follows Black Hawk's Rock River from the south edges of Rockford to Dixon, through a valley whose current residents love their towns, cornfields, and homes as much as Black Hawk did. It is still beautiful country where woodlands frame limestone bluffs that press against the river, opening into vistas of subtly rolling hills and farm fields. In Black Hawk's day, the Rock River cut through seemingly

15

endless prairies, whose sticky loam discouraged pioneers using old-fashioned plows—until in 1837 a blacksmith named John Deere in the river town of Grand Detour invented a polished steel plow that cleanly sliced the rich midwestern soil.

By the early 1900s, some of Chicago's rich and powerful families had built grand summer spreads along this section of the valley, enlivened by a thriving art colony. And down in Dixon, Ronald Reagan was spending his boyhood years in a thoroughly middle-class home. These days, the family-style sights and activities along the Rock River retain the wholesome feel of yesteryear.

Rockford, the second largest city in Illinois, took its name from the ford across the Rock River used by stagecoaches on the Chicago–Galena run. As it fans out from the winding river, Rockford offers plenty of sightseeing stops: the Time Museum of clocks and timekeeping devices; the Burpee Museum of Natural History, featuring wildlife, fossils, minerals, and Indian artifacts; Sinnissippi botanical gardens; and the 1865 Tinker Swiss Cottage, a twenty-room Victorian version of a mountain chalet.

We head south from the city on Route 2 and stay on that river-hugging road to Dixon. Almost immediately after crossing the four-lane US 20 that bands Rockford's belly, forests close in along the road and riverbank as a buffer from the urban strip malls and gas stations.

The Rock is clearly a river—not just a creek pretending to be bigger than its britches—but it's much cozier than the mighty Mississippi into which it flows. You can study its opposite shore with the naked eye instead of powerful binoculars.

At first, an occasional trailer park or modern development can be glimpsed through the trees. Further on, gentle waves of green farm fields roll away from the river. Shaded pullouts are common, frequented by picnickers, fishermen, boaters, and canoeists. Birdwatchers, too, can observe the resident ducks and other feathered friends on the points of the narrow, wooded islands that stud the water.

Then the bluffs close in—cliffs of layered sedimentary stone formed half a million years ago when all this was the

Along the Rock River

bottom of a warm, shallow sea. Later the earth's crust bowed, tilted and faulted the rocks, and massive tongues of ice shoved and scraped the landscape. Erosion wore holes in the thin blanket of soil, revealing patches of the oldest exposed rock material in Illinois: 500-million-year-old dolomite, a compact limestone bedrock, and the somewhat younger St. Peter sandstone.

The cliffs part for a glimpse of black angus grazing inside white-fenced Rock River Farms. Back in 1912, the 1,800-acre farm was purchased by Ruth and Medill McCormick shortly after he left the family-owned *Chicago Tribune*. (His older brother, the controversial Colonel Robert McCormick, became publisher; Medill was later elected to the U.S. Senate.) When the McCormicks owned it, Rock River Farms was one of the nation's premier breeders of Holstein cattle.

Just before the town of Byron, you can pay a daily fee to swim and picnic at spring-fed Lake Louise. This thirteen-acre, beach-lined lake is part of a privately owned recreational vehicle park where you'll also find rowboats for rent, fishing, horseshoe pits, a game arcade, and a snack bar.

Byron was called Bloomingville when it was founded by New Englanders in 1835. Late in the century, residents swept up in admiration for the English poet Lord Byron changed the town's name. During the Civil War, Byron was an active abolitionist center, and many residents offered their homes and farms as Underground Railroad stations. The 1866 Civil War monument at Chestnut and Second streets was the first such memorial in the state; the names of those who served are almost worn off the small obelisk.

Byron is now a tidy river town. The American Legion chapter has moved into a once-vacant movie theater. The Byron Boat Basin rents canoes for day trips from Rockford to Oregon (a nearby town, not the state). Busy Byronites have erected a handsome dark wood library, and are restoring as a visitors center the 1836 Greek Revival Lucius Read House, the second oldest home in the village.

Cross the river on Route 72 and turn south (right) on River Road. Almost immediately, you'll turn left to reach the 450-acre Jarrett Prairie Center on a hilltop above a golf course. There the Byron Forest Preserve District is restoring the native grasslands of a dolomite hill prairie, which grows on the thin layer of soil covering the ancient limestone bedrock.

On a sunny, seventy-degree June day, I visited Jarrett and admired the illuminating exhibits on prairie life in the visitors center, as well as the gentle way its naturalist introduced a local snake and a youngster to one another. At the start of an easygoing trail, labels pointed out the sky blue aster, little bluestem, prairie rose, and other native plants. A dozen or more indigo buntings flitted among the bushes and trees at the edge of the prairie, their deep blue feathers more dazzling than any jewel I've ever seen. Crickets and warblers provided a background chorus, with the "tzt-tzt-tzt" call of field sparrows for a rhythm section.

In 1839, J.H. Smith wrote of this nearly treeless landscape: "The prairies in the summer present one vast natural garden of delights spreading before the eye such a beautiful and variegated scenery decked with flowers of every shape, size, and hue, that he that could not admire them must be destitute of a sense of beauty and elegance." Smith was correct.

Several miles further east on Route 72 lies Stillman Valley, a cheerful and growing small town named for Major Isiah Stillman, who led 275 men into the first battle of the Black Hawk War on May 14, 1832. A fifty-foot granite obelisk, topped by a figure of a citizen soldier, honors the twelve soldiers killed in the battle; nine are buried on the site, their graves marked by simple headstones.

Back on Route 2 south of Byron, the road levels off and hills rise west of the highway. Small boats perch on the riverbank next to compact homes. Across the river, steam rises from the Byron Nuclear Plant's cooling towers.

A roadside historical marker along this stretch reminds passersby that Illinois was once America's Wild West—complete with gun-toting criminals and frontier justice. In the 1830s and 1840s, a gang of horse thieves and murderers called the Banditti of the Prairie operated along the Rock River. After six members were jailed in Oregon in March 1841, the new courthouse there was torched. A vigilante group called the Regulators formed and ordered suspected Banditti, including John Driscoll and his four sons, to high-tail it or be whipped. The Driscolls responded by killing the leader of the Regulators, who promptly captured the Banditti family and put them on trial before a Regulator judge and a 111-man jury. John and one son were found guilty and shot. Three months later, the 112 Regulators were tried and acquitted of murder in Ogle County circuit court.

Near the Leaf River, Route 2 curves through hills then skirts beneath high bluffs. Up above sits the castlelike Stronghold, built just after the stock market crash in 1929 by Walter Strong, publisher of the *Chicago Daily News*. It is said that Strong was fulfilling a boyhood dream of living in a medieval European castle. The interior contains a great hall, a tower, and a secret passageway to a hidden chapel. The Stronghold is now a Presbyterian conference and retreat center only open to the public during Oregon's Autumn on Parade festival each October. But you can drive up the hill to view the exterior any day before 4:00 P.M.

As the river valley widens, you'll spot the massive statue of a Native American rising majestically from the heavily wooded bluffs across the river. This fifty-foot-high, concrete-reinforced sculpture was designed by Lorado Taft as a general tribute to the American Indian, though everyone calls it Black Hawk. It stands in Lowden State Park, which we'll visit later. Just across from the statue is Maxson Manor, a restaurant well known in the region. In 1950, Bob Maxson opened it in this 1898 chalet-style summer home built by a Chicago industrialist. "You can sit by the river there and watch the boats and ducks and birds with the Black Hawk statue in the background," said Maxson, who sold the restaurant when he retired several years ago.

"Years before the go-fast roads, this was the turnaround point for Sunday drives for people from Oak Park and other south- and west-Chicago suburbs," he went on. "They'd come out here, have a nice lunch, and return." The new owners have maintained the quality of food and service at the restaurant while adding a 109-foot paddlewheel boat for lunch, dinner, and sightseeing cruises.

Oregon is an easygoing county seat with a fine Lorado Taft Soldiers Monument on its courthouse lawn. Decker Drugs downtown has a 1950s-style soda fountain. The 1893 brick piano factory at Third and Franklin streets now houses a dozen or more antique and specialty shops, and a pair of handsome Victorian mansions, Lyndel and Pinehill, have been turned into bed and breakfast inns.

Cross the Rock River on Route 64 and turn north (left) on River Road to Lowden State Park, a fine picnicking and camping spot. I remember some great games of tag with my cousins up on these bluffs, my great-grandmother beaming at us from the picnic table.

In 1843, Concord Group poet Margaret Fuller wrote "Ganymede to His Eagle" here, inspired by an eagle roost high above the river. In 1898, Wallace Heckman, attorney and business manager of the University of Chicago, bought the property and called it Ganymede Farm. Heckman, a patron of the arts, devoted fifteen of the farm's acres to an artist's colony called Eagle's Nest, which lasted until 1942 when the last of its original members died. The colony's moving spirit was sculptor Lorado Taft, whose works had graced Chicago's 1893 World's Columbian Exposition. Members also included organist Clarence Dickerson, nature writer Hamlin Garland, and other artists, architects, and writers. They worked and socialized here each summer, occupying cottages and a lodge with sixteen-inch-thick stone walls. Located next to the park, those buildings now comprise Northern Illinois University's Lorado Taft Field Campus for outdoor education.

About four miles of trails wind through the park, including one that zigzags from the feet of the Black Hawk statue down the steep bluff to the river. If this monument to Native Americans looks mighty like a paleface, it's because Hamlin Garland was its model. Other works of the art colony can be seen on request at the Oregon Public Library any afternoon but Sunday.

Sinnissippi Forest, one of the largest Christmas tree farms in the state, lies south of Lowden State Park. Return from Lowden to Route 64, turn east (left) to Daysville Road, then south (right); keep to the right as Daysville Road becomes Lowden Road. Almost 300 acres owned by Warren and Nancy Miller are devoted to raising prize-winning Christmas trees. You can cut your own tree or choose one already felled. Hay-wagon tours through the forest to a pick-a-pumpkin patch are run during Oregon's Autumn on Parade festival.

Frank Lowden, who served as governor of Illinois during World War I, purchased this area at the turn of the century, and it was the state's first tree farm. The Millers, who are his heirs, sold about 1,200 acres of the original land to Illinois in 1992 to create a new state forest that includes several miles of Rock River shoreline, wetlands, two islands, pine plantations, and native hardwood stands.

Return to downtown Oregon and go south (left) on Route 2 to Pines Road, where you turn west (right) toward White Pines Forest State Park and other old-time, pre-Disney family attractions. The road travels among farms and past a seasonal produce market or two before turning south (left) onto Ridge Road, then west (right) onto Pines Road again. At this jog is the 300-acre White Pines Ranch, a dude ranch for kids and teenagers with a hundred head of cattle plus another hundred horses, mules, ponies, pigs, cats, and dogs. You can rent horses here for trail rides.

At a wooded intersection further along is the privately-owned White Pines Deer Park, open May through September, where almost 200 deer wander through the forest waiting to be fed by visitors or the park's owners. The park also includes a small zoo, pony and wagon rides, a half-mile train, a picnic area, and other entertainment aimed at younger children.

Two miles beyond is the entrance to White Pines Forest State Park, a 365-acre plot with the southernmost stand of white pines left in the United States. Park roads ford shallow creeks that have carved through the limestone bedrock. The recently renovated lodge and cabins were constructed of logs and limestone by the Civilian Conservation Corps in the 1930s. In the summer, the lodge presents a dinner theater schedule of musicals. Just outside the park sits a roller-skating rink and Ken's Clock Shop, a flea market of antiques, snacks, ice, bait, and wood.

Return to Route 2. South of Oregon, the road climbs over wooded hills, then passes beneath rock formations to Castle Rock, a 150-foot summit of the fragile St. Peter sandstone inside Castle Rock State Park. Climb the wooden stairs to the top of the rock for a wide view of the island-studded river. Directly across the water is Sinnissippi Farms and the new state forest. Other trails lead inland through ravines and rolling hills.

At Grand Detour, five and a half miles further on, the river U-turns into a horseshoe bend so that the town fronts the water on two sides. In 1836, Major Leonard Andrus arrived here with settlers from Vermont. Andrus erected a dam and mills, began work on the river road from Dixon to Rockford, and formed stage lines. In 1837, Vermont blacksmith John Deere came to town and set up his forge. As he shoed horses and fashioned hay forks and shovels, he learned of the struggles farmers faced trying to carve prairie soil with their cast-iron and wooden plows. The rich loam was so sticky that farmers had to stop and scrape their plows every few feet. To help them, Deere invented a highly polished plow of stainless steel that shed the soil and proved the key to the successful cultivation of the Midwest. Deere, in partnership with Andrus, opened a plow factory in Grand Detour, and in 1847 moved to Moline to open a second plant.

As you reach Grand Detour, you might hear the clang of hammer on steel coming from a replica of Deere's blacksmith shop. Nearby is the home he built in 1836 and a neighbor's house that serves as a visitors center. The group of buildings, set on a shady square block surrounded by a white picket fence, is open April through November. A patch of restored prairie grows between the highway and the historic site.

Stroll or drive through the rest of the hamlet. Minus automobiles, TV antennas, and other modern paraphernalia, you'd swear you'd stepped into a quiet, nineteenth-century farm town. The 1849 St. Peter's Episcopal Church is on land donated by Andrus. Homes sit far back from the street on wide, shady lots, and one or two are now bed and breakfasts.

Route 2 crosses the river as it begins its own "grand detour," then cuts across wooded hilltops overlooking flat cornfields before reaching Dixon. In the center of town half a block south of Route 2, a victory arch rises over Galena Avenue to honor World War I veterans. Near its base stands the Nachusa House hotel, built in 1837, which claims to have added a bathtub even before the White House had one. Five U.S. presidents stayed here—Abraham Lincoln, Ulysses S. Grant, Theodore Roosevelt, William Howard Taft, and Ronald Reagan—but now it's shuttered and hopeful of restoration.

In December 1920, Jack Reagan, a lifelong Democrat, moved his family into the modest white-frame home at 816 S. Hennepin Avenue from Tampico, where his son Ronald had been born nine years earlier. As boys, "Dutch" Reagan and his brother Neil, known as "Moon," raised rabbits and played football. Later, Dutch worked as a lifeguard at Lowell Park north of Dixon and served on the 1928 high school yearbook staff. His house is open for guided tours. Next door stands a bronze statue of Ronald Reagan holding seed corn in his hand.

Follow Route 2/US 52 across the Rock River and turn left to the site of Fort Dixon. A statue of young Abraham Lincoln, who arrived here in the summer of 1832 as a captain in the Black Hawk War, looks out over the Rock River. Like Black Hawk and the other Native Americans who preceded him in Illinois, Lincoln loved this beautiful country.

In the Area

All numbers are in area code 815.

Northern Illinois Tourism Council, 150 N. Ninth Street, Rockford, IL 61107: 964-6482 or 800-248-6482

Rock River Valley Convention and Tourism Bureau (Polo): 946-2108

Oregon Chamber of Commerce: 732-2100

Byron Chamber of Commerce: 234-5900

Dixon Chamber of Commerce: 284-3361

Lake Louise Camping Resort (Byron): 234-8483

Jarrett Prairie Center (Byron): 234-8535

The Stronghold (Oregon): 732-6111

Maxson Manor (Oregon): 800-468-4222

Oregon Public Library: 732-2724

Lyndel Mansion Bed and Breakfast and Tea Room (Oregon):
732-7313

Pinehill Bed and Breakfast (Oregon): 732-2061

Lowden State Park (Oregon): 732-6828

Sinnissippi Forest (Oregon): 732-6240

White Pines Forest State Park (Mount Morris): 946-3717

White Pines Inn (Mount Morris): 946-3817

White Pines Ranch (Oregon): 732-7923

White Pines Deer Park (Oregon): 732-2088

Castle Rock State Park (Oregon): 732-7329

John Deere Historic Site (Grand Detour): 652-4551

Ronald Reagan Boyhood Home (Dixon): 288-3404

3 ~

The Fox River Valley

To get there, take I-94 (the Tri-State Tollway) north from Chicago for about 50 miles. Exit west on Route 173 to Antioch. This trip focuses on the Fox Lake area; you can take any east–west highway back to I-94.

Highlights: *Antioch; Chain O' Lakes State Park, Moraine Hills State Park, and Volo Bog State Natural Area; antique stores, galleries, and homemade candy in Richmond; Harvard, the "Milk Center of the World"; Seven Acres Antique Village and Wild West Town, Illinois Railway Museum, and Woodstock Opera House.*

The glacier-carved terrain of northeastern Illinois conceals everything from a quaking bog and creamy chocolates to comic-strip character Dick Tracy. They're all tucked in around the Chain O' Lakes (ten of them) fed by the Fox River in a population-pressed region of wetlands, low hills, and rich plains. Although Chicago's suburbia is bulldozing its way into parts of this route, there's still plenty of country left to be enjoyed. Outdoors-oriented weekenders pack the Fox River Valley during warm weather, so travel its roads in midweek or in cooler seasons if you prefer a quieter journey.

Antioch, an old resort town abutting the Wisconsin border, is our starting point. As you drive toward it on Route 173, you'll edge into the country past marshes sprouting cattails, horse and pony farms, and vegetable stands typical of what you'll find all along this circuit. One roadside market sells hot dogs and Italian beef sandwiches in addition to carrots and zucchini. This part of Illinois abounds in market gardens. It's horse country, too: McHenry County, just west of Antioch, has an equine population of 10,000.

Antioch's heart is ringed by the neon cholesterol of fast-food restaurants and strip malls. But the old downtown, just north on Route 83, remains a thriving small-town mix of clothing shops, cafés, and drugstores. The most picturesque spot to stretch your legs is the Hiram Buttrick Mill northwest of city hall. This photogenic replica of an 1839 sawmill sits above a pond in a pretty, peaceful park.

In 1843, the village's religious majority named their community after the Asia Minor city where the disciples of Christ were first called Christians. But the original Antioch was also a noted pleasure capital, and its Illinois namesake followed in those footsteps. By 1900, summer resorts and cottages were strung along the shores of the surrounding lakes. Every summer, crowds of tourists boated among the tall waxy-yellow blooms of American lotus that clogged shallow Grass Lake and perfumed the air for miles around. Some clumps of lotus still grow along the lake's edge.

Continue west on Route 173 along a jumble of small lakes, marinas, cottages in the woods, campsites, and taverns like Vi's Yellow Bird, which packs an enthusiastic crowd onto its dance floor on weekends. This old-time recreation area looks both shopworn and cheerful—like an aging waitress who knows every joke in the world and still loves to tell them.

Just past a wide marsh, a left turn leads into the northern end of Chain O' Lakes State Park, which lies beside the Fox River. You might spot deer moving soundlessly across the landscape, especially early in the day. This is the quieter end of the park—at least until an access road is pushed through from its southern sector, an area crammed with boaters and picnicking families in the warm-weather months.

Toward Richmond, the landscape dries and begins to undulate. You'll start seeing farms, mostly growing crops or cattle, some devoted to horses, and one raising pheasants for the pleasure of hunters and diners. In Richmond, turn south on US 12 (Main Street). Elder's Mill is a restaurant and gallery with a history. Located in what was once the sales and storage building of an 1844 mill, it has shifted from grinding grain to dishing up hearty French cuisine. Tradition has it that the first person who climbed to the top of the mill (the foundation is all that remains) got to name the town.

The corner of Main and Broadway is the center of Richmond's business district, captured by antique stores and galleries. Twenty-five years ago, Richmond's downtown was run-down and dumpy—until a local realtor paid attention to his mother's fortune teller, who envisioned seventeen antique shops there. The realtor got busy and now you'll find at least that number, offering big-city selections at small-town prices. A few of the best are: A Little Bit Antiques (the name describes its varied stock); Antiques on Broadway, which impressed me with its finely restored furniture; the 1905 Emporium, a former drugstore and soda fountain with everything from antique toys to ancient toothbrushes packed floor to ceiling; and Ed's Antiques, where exquisite stained and leaded glass caught my eye.

Your nose may lead you on down Main Street to Anderson's Homemade Candies, where they use cream from a local farm to make the scrumptious chocolates. Raynold Anderson's father started the company in Chicago in 1919 and moved to Richmond in 1926 when the rent got too high. The shop had to close during World War II because of sugar and chocolate shortages, but Raynold got it up and running again—with former customers waiting on the doorstep—after he was discharged from the service. His sons, Leif and Lars, operate it now in an enclosed porch of the house their grandfather bought almost seventy years ago. A cheerful saleslady convinced me that eating a pound of chocolate a day is good for you.

Head west again on Route 173 through Hebron, whose high point is a water tower painted like a basketball in honor of its long-ago 1952 state champions. Further on, prosperous-looking farms mingle with abandoned barns and brand-new homes, marking the transition from small homesteads to large farms to creeping suburbia. Nip through Alden and Dynamite Springs into Harvard.

Standing in the middle of this community's main intersection is a guaranteed double take: a three-quarter-size black-and-white cow named Harmilda. Harvard is the "Milk Center of the World," according to a sign on Harmilda's pedestal. Well, yes and no. In 1942, when seven dairy companies were located within fifteen miles of Harvard, more milk was being produced here than anywhere else in the country. But now all the dairies have moved or closed, and counties further west in Illinois and elsewhere in the U.S. have taken the lead in milk production.

Plenty of cows are still out in the fields around Harvard, however, and the townspeople continue to honor their bovines during "Harvard Milk Days" the first weekend each June. It's a real country-style event with a two-hour parade, cattle and horse shows, a truck/tractor pull, and farm tours.

At Harmilda's corner, turn south (left) into downtown Harvard and stroll by some shops that have been in business a while. See if you can resist the sweet rolls and Swedish limpa bread at the fourth-generation Swiss Maid Bakery on Brainerd Street. Bopp's Tavern on Front Street is a fifty-year-old farmer-style family place. And stick your head into Jerry Nolan's barber shop, Harvard's social center along N. Ayer Street, to see his eighty-year-old chair. You'll also spot Roach's Hardware near the train tracks: "If we don't have it, you don't want it," Roach's proclaims.

Go south out of Harvard on US 14 and turn right toward Marengo on Route 23 just before the Heritage House Restaurant. Head south past horse farms, cornfields, and Holsteins.

Harmilda the Holstein greets visitors to Harvard

In addition to the live cows, many farmhouses sport knee-high plastic models as lawn ornaments.

When you reach Marengo, turn east (left) off Route 23 onto US 20 past well-manicured Victorian homes that show how prosperous these farm communities were at the turn of the century. Go through town and stay tuned for a left turn at a sign pointing toward Union, population 650. Before you reach Union village, you'll see a right-turn sign to Seven Acres Antique Village and Wild West Town, an unabashedly pre-Disney theme park with everything from cowboy gunfights near the Old Union Jail to an antique phonograph collection and old-timey shops.

In Union, go straight ahead at its stop sign, on past a barbecue-sauce factory, and around a corner to the village's pièce de résistance, the living-history Illinois Railway Museum. Here you'll see hundreds of railroad coaches, steam and diesel engines, old city streetcars, trolleys, interurbans, and other memorabilia. In summer, the old trains chug and clack along the tracks.

Return from the Railway Museum to Main Street and turn north (right); you're heading the correct direction if the McHenry County Historical Museum, in an 1870s school building, is on your right. Go a mile or so to Route 176 and turn east (right). The countryside has flattened out here into crop-growing fields.

Turn north (left) on Route 47 toward Woodstock, named by settlers in the 1830s and 1840s for the Vermont community from which they'd begun their westward migration. Wood-stock's shady Victorian town square is graced by a bandstand and spring house and lined by brick streets. It is the scene of ice cream socials, craft shows, and, each Wednesday in season, a farmers market and band concert. The buildings around it have been so lovingly restored that you can almost believe horseless carriages haven't yet been invented.

The Woodstock Opera House, facing the square, was built in 1889 as a combination fire department, city hall, public library, and auditorium. Restored in 1977, its interior decor is functional, not gilt-stricken like many other Victorian opera houses and 1920s movie theaters. A resident ghost makes up for the theater's plain-Jane look, the specter of a young woman who hung herself when rebuffed by a handsome young performer.

Kitty-corner across the square, the former county courthouse boasts a small museum dedicated to Chester Gould, creator of the Dick Tracy comic strip and a fifty-year resident of Woodstock. Inside is the drawing board where Gould sketched the strong-jawed detective with the two-way wrist radio.

Leave Woodstock on US 14 south, and when you come to Route 176, go east (left). You'll soon enter more heavily populated territory, but don't lose heart. Continue past the older homes on the northern fringes of Crystal Lake, a nineteenth-century town engulfed by the Chicago metropolis only in recent years. Across Route 31, suburbia continues to horn in on farm fields and forest remnants until you reach River Road.

Horse-lovers should take the time for a side trip here: at River Road, continue a short distance on Route 176 to Roberts Road where you turn south (right). Look for Timmermann's Ranch and Saddle Shop on your left. For about thirty-five years, the Timmermann family has been raising, training, selling, and boarding horses, as well as teaching riding in indoor and outdoor arenas. Their shop is crammed with saddles, horse-care products, and Western wear. I stopped to check out their cowboy boots, elaborate silver belt buckles, and fringed shirts.

"We just had a foal," Mrs. Timmermann told me when I was done browsing. "Go on over to the barn and see her." I was impressed not only with the cocoa-colored filly's cuteness, but also with the gentle way she and her mother were handled by a soft-spoken hand who let me slip behind him into the stall for a closer look.

After your detour, return to Route 176 and go back to River Road. Turn north on River Road and it's not far to the entrance to Moraine Hills State Park. The park's most popular spot is a picnic grove and fishing hole next to McHenry Dam on the Fox River. My favorite walk here traverses a short, easy trail and a floating boardwalk at 115-acre Pike Marsh. The marsh is in the depression left when a huge glacial ice block melted. It's bounded by moraine hills made of boulders, stones, and other debris deposited by the Ice Age glaciers.

A trail guide helps you pick out (but please don't pick) plants like the red-flowered joe-pye weed, with its triangular stems and whorled leaves, or bog-dwelling beauties such as the marsh cinquefoil and silver-leaved hoary willow. Pitcher plants that trap and digest insects thrive here. Cattails also do well—too well—and we can thank the muskrats who fell them for food and housing for helping to keep them under control. You'll see the rodents' domed, thatch-roofed homes scattered through the bog.

Continue north on River Road to Route 120 and turn east (right), traveling briefly through a strip of small malls and gas stations. By the time you reach Krueger's Farm, another road-side stand and U-pick spot, you're back in the country . . . until you bump up against four-lane US 12/Route 59 at Volo.

Turn north (left), keeping your eyes peeled for small brown signs pointing you west (left) to the Volo Bog State Natural Area. You get two chances: on Sullivan Lake Road or further north on Big Hollow Road. Volo Bog differs somewhat from the marsh wetland and bog at Moraine Hills. It centers on a *quaking* bog, a floating mat composed of sphagnum moss, cattails, and sedges surrounding an open pool of water. Next is a ring of poison sumac and leatherleaf shrubs, then a forest of tamarack (known in some areas as larch). Surrounding this is a larger shrub community that abruptly gives way to a marsh meadow growing from soft, saturated muck.

At the visitors center, pick up a seasonal guide to the half-mile trail or ask whether the naturalist is leading a walk that day. Either one will help you discover the subtle things among the changing vegetation. In fall, you might spot a monarch butterfly caterpillar, black with white and yellow bands. In winter, a weasel might have left tracks across the snow toward its den. In spring, red-winged blackbirds will be churring and squawking to stake out nesting territories. Such wetlands used to be viewed as loathsome places best filled in. Only in recent years have we learned how they help reduce flooding and filter pollutants from the water flowing through them.

Our route ends at this wetland remnant. US 12/Route 59 will take you north again to Antioch or to east–west highways leading back to I-94.

In the Area

Northern Illinois Tourism Council, 150 N. Ninth Street, Rockford, IL 61107: 815-964-6482 or 800-248-6482

Elgin Area Convention and Visitors Bureau (covers Marengo and Union): 708-741-5660

Lake County Convention and Visitors Bureau: 708-662-2700 or 800-525-3669

Antioch Chamber of Commerce: 708-395-2233

Chain O' Lakes State Park (Antioch): 708-587-5512

Elder's Mill Restaurant and Art Gallery (Richmond): 815-678-2841

Anderson's Homemade Candies (Richmond): 815-678-4030

McHenry County Conservation District (Ringwood): 815-678-4431

Greater Harvard Chamber of Commerce: 815-943-4404

Woodstock Chamber of Commerce: 815-338-2436

McHenry Chamber of Commerce: 815-385-4301

Seven Acres Antique Village and Wild West Town (Union):
815-923-2214

McHenry County Historical Museum (Union): 815-923-2267

Illinois Railway Museum (Union): 800-244-7245

Woodstock Opera House: 815-338-5300

Timmermann's Ranch and Saddle Shop (Island Lake):
708-526-8066

Moraine Hills State Park (McHenry): 815-385-1624

Krueger's Farm (McHenry): 815-385-4981

Volo Bog State Natural Area (Ingleside): 815-344-1294

4 ~

The Illinois & Michigan Canal

To get there, take I-55 southwest from Chicago; exit at Route 83 south. This trip runs west along the Illinois & Michigan Canal to La Salle.

Highlights: *St. James of the Sag Church; Strand Antique Emporium & Ice Cream Parlor; I&M Canal Museum and Gaylord Building in Lockport; I&M Canal State Trail, Goose Lake Prairie State Natural Area, Starved Rock State Park, and Matthiessen State Park; Ottawa, site of the first Lincoln-Douglas debate.*

The Illinois & Michigan Canal opened the upper Midwest to pioneers and commerce by providing the first navigable passageway between the Great Lakes and the Mississippi River. It played a major role in Chicago's extraordinary growth into the transportation and commercial hub of the region. The canal first opened its locks in 1848 along a ninety-seven-mile corridor that started at the Chicago River in Chicago and connected with the Illinois River at La Salle and Peru.

Speedier railroads eventually sucked away much of the I&M's traffic; a wider, deeper canal through the Chicago metropolitan area, completed in 1900, finished it off. The I&M

became hidden by foliage, clogged by debris, and was partially filled in. But along its banks, forests, wetlands, and remnants of prairies survive in nearly fifty parks and preserves spaced through a sprawl of refineries, cornfields, and quarries.

Some of the old canal towns dozed off for some years, but started to reawaken after Congress named the I&M corridor the nation's first National Linear Park in 1984. That designation spurred the restoration and tidying up of towpaths, trails, and nineteenth-century buildings along the narrow waterway. In this noisy era of jet planes and giant trucks, many stretches of the canal are astonishingly quiet—just as they were in the last century when only the sound of mules along the towpath or chatting boatmen broke the stillness.

A complete route along the Illinois & Michigan Canal would begin at the Chicago River in the middle of the city, then thread through densely packed suburbs before emerging onto country roads. Instead, zip out of the metropolitan jungle on I-55, getting off at exit 247 to go south on Route 83 (Robert Kingery Highway). You've entered an urban twilight zone. As you cross the Des Plaines River and the Chicago Sanitary & Ship Canal—the I&M's successor—acres of auto junkyards are spread below. At a stoplight just across the bridge, turn left onto Archer Avenue (Route 171). Follow Route 171 a short distance to the right turn leading up a steep hill to St. James of the Sag Church and cemetery.

Here you can tip your hat to the Irish immigrants who labored on the I&M Canal. On their one day off a week, they built this graceful church in the 1830s from native limestone; it is the oldest active Roman Catholic parish in the Chicago diocese.

Folksinger Kevin O'Donnell, a member of the group Arranmore, wrote a song about these workers, part of which goes:

So bid farewell to famine, it's off to Americay
To work as a navigator for ninety cents a day.
And hope to dig a fortune by the time they reach La Salle
On the Illinois and Michigan Canal.

Hundreds of Irish workers died while building the I&M and some are buried in the St. James cemetery.

Return to the stoplight, turn south (left), and go a short distance to a second stoplight. Turn right onto Chicago-Joliet Road toward Lemont, passing canal-era legacies of quarries and Catholic schools, convents and retreats. You'll enter Lemont on Main Street. At its Historical Society Museum, a block and a half uphill on Lemont Street in an 1861 limestone church, I learned that those wonderful tin ceilings you see in country stores and taverns were invented here. It seems that the blasting going on at all the quarries in the area cracked the plaster in local buildings, so an enterprising hardware-store family patented and manufactured embossed metal ceilings to cover the cracks—and became quite wealthy. An example of a patterned metal ceiling is in the church that houses the museum.

Return to Main Street and backtrack one block to Stephen Street. Turn left and cross the railroad tracks into Lemont's old downtown of sturdy limestone and wood frame buildings along the I&M. Start your tour down by the canal, which looks much the same as it did in 1848 because its sides and bottom are made of limestone bedrock. Cutting through that was the final step in completing the canal. Packet boats passed by three times a day during their twenty-two-hour journey from Chicago to La Salle, pulled in early years by horses or mules; tickets then cost $4.00.

Much of the small downtown is either occupied by old-time businesses or has been recently restored. It hasn't given itself over to cutesy gift shops and fudge factories—though it may sound that way when you pass the Cookie Jar Museum (with 2,000 or more containers) or the Christmas Inn, a tavern where it's December 25th year-round.

My favorite spot is the Strand Antique Emporium and Ice Cream Parlor in the 1870 Norton Building alongside the canal. Inside, you pass a counter area to dark wood booths and tables with a few antiques set out on old bookcases and sideboards. The menu ranges from an asparagus appetizer to meatloaf sandwiches, fried squid, and hearty German specials. Your teeth may ache just reading the ice cream menu. Or you might rather sink your teeth into a hamburger from Nick's Tavern at 221 Main Street. Nick's is famous for its one-pound slabs of hamburger. This is not fast food; it takes fifteen minutes to cook them up.

Lemont also has its share of antique shops. A large antique tool collection is displayed high on one long wall of the Ace Hardware at 225 Canal Street, where you'll also find beaded purses, old hand grenades, and other collectible stuff jumbled in with the usual hardware-store mix of nails and toasters.

Leave Lemont on Main Street, which changes names faster than a fleeing con artist. It joins Lemont Road, then Route 171, and becomes State Street in Lockport, established as the headquarters for the I&M Canal. Turn right on 8th Street and park. Across the railroad tracks is the Illinois & Michigan Canal Visitors Center inside the handsomely restored Gaylord Building, three stories with arched windows in the golden-yellow native limestone. Originally a general store, the 1859 Gaylord Building abuts an 1838 warehouse built when canal construction began; the warehouse is now home to the Public Landing Restaurant.

Back on the corner of 8th and State streets, a frame building served as canal offices and the home of commissioners. Now it's the Will County Historical Society's ten-room Illinois

& Michigan Canal Museum full of canal-era memorabilia like the first commissioner's rolltop desk, bedroom furniture made by Swedes, an Irish cradle, and so on.

Behind the museum and outside the Gaylord Building, a pioneer settlement of more than a dozen buildings provides a glimpse of rural life during the canal's early days. Walk through the settlement and along the canal towpath for half a mile to reach Lock #1, the first of fifteen used to raise and lower boats.

Leaving Lockport on Route 171, you're faced with the city of Joliet—77,000 strong. Some of its historic downtown buildings have been restored, including the Rialto Square Theater, a gilded 1920s masterpiece with a crystal chandelier heavy enough to sink an I&M steamboat. But unless you arrive on a Tuesday at 12:45 P.M. when tours are offered, keep following Route 171 until it meets US 6, which you take west. The industrial grit will ease as you reach Channahon. Cross the I&M, then follow a sign pointing left to the Channahon access to the I&M Canal State Trail.

In the photogenic park, Lock #6 spills into the Des Plaines River below a restored lock tender's house. Just across the river above a spillway, Lock #7 leads back into the canal channel. Since the locking process took fifteen minutes, this may have been a spot for traffic jams. Between here and La Salle, hikers can stride along a sixty-mile stretch of towpath, sections of which have been surfaced for biking. (Trails along the canal total more than seventy-five miles and maps are available at the ranger station.)

The easiest way to reach Morris, our next destination, is to return to busy US 6 and continue west. But there's also a slower country route that runs along the canal. The directions sound complicated, but the drive is pretty and worth the effort. As you leave the park at Lock #6, turn right on Canal

The Illinois & Michigan Canal

Street instead of left back to US 6. Go to Bridge Street and turn right, crossing the DuPage River and canal. Continue about a mile. When you see a farmhouse and trailer on your left, angle left. Very shortly, you'll reach an unmarked intersection with McKinley Road (it leads to the canal-side McKinley

Woods Forest Preserve). You can see US 6 off to your right. Keep going straight on Hansel Road, which crosses flat farmlands before leading downhill to the canal. Tiny Dresden Cemetery will be on your right. The huge Dresden power plant rears up across the river. When you reach a stop sign, turn left. The road crosses the canal at the Dresden trail-access point. Along this stretch the DuPage, Des Plaines, and Kankakee rivers join to form the Illinois River.

The blacktop is now called Cemetery Road and leads past farm fields and grassy patches on the river's bottomlands. Another trail-access point is at Lock #8, a peaceful spot where you'll find a restored lock tender's house and an aqueduct that carries the canal across Aux Sable Creek. Reach it by going right over the canal on Tabler Road, then left on Dellos Road to the parking lot.

At the edge of Morris, the blacktop goes left around Evergreen Cemetery. Buried here is Potawatomi Chief Shabbona, who in 1832 refused to join Black Hawk in his war against invading pioneers and tried to warn the settlers of the impending attack; fifteen who did not flee were killed at the Indian Creek Massacre. A town and state park north of here were named in his honor. Cemetery Road becomes Armstrong Street and passes a former train station and grain elevator, ducks under Route 47, and U-turns to intersect with it. The old downtown lies west of Route 47; the town's new strip is north toward US 6 and I-80.

For a bite to eat in Morris, try Weits Cafe, 213 Liberty Street. Stop in at this local favorite for homemade pie, Sunday brunch, or a full meal. If you prefer a more upscale establishment, it's worth going to the Rockwell Inn, 2400 US Route 6 West just to see the handsome dark wood bar backed by arched mirrors that were made for Anheuser-Busch Breweries for Chicago's 1893 World's Columbian Exposition. The cooking is excellent; coat and tie are not required.

To find the largest piece of prairie left in Illinois, take a side trip. Go south on Route 47 across the Illinois River, then east (left) on Pine Bluff/Lorenzo Road. Turn left (north) at Jugtown Road, off which is the visitors center for the 2,537-acre Goose Lake Prairie State Natural Area. When the first pioneers arrived, two-thirds of Illinois was covered by prairies, earning it the nickname "The Prairie State"; only about one-half of one percent of the original grasslands remain now. Here, however, you can still get a feel for the vastness of the prairie that once stretched to the foothills of the Rockies. Early settlers described the unfamiliar landscape as "a sea of grass," some of which reached eight to twelve feet high.

Loop trails lead through the largest stand of tall grass prairie left in the state, a lush wildflower-bedecked landscape that is a nesting habitat for rare birds such as the upland sandpiper and Henslow's sparrow, and a home for deer, coyotes, red foxes, beavers, and other wildlife. The paths wind past ponds and prairie marshes and to the top of a strip mine spoil mound. When you first arrive, nearby power plants and high-tension wires seem intrusive; once you're out on the paths, it's easy to get absorbed in the beauty of the prairie.

Take route 47 back into Morris, then take Jefferson Street west. It becomes Ottawa Street, leading to Gebhard Woods, a little gem tucked between Nettle Creek and a restored stretch of the canal. Picnic areas and ponds are nestled among stately old walnut, oak, and maple trees.

Ottawa Street changes its name to Old Stage Road, a narrow blacktop through sparsely populated countryside. You'll cross the I&M on a one-lane bridge next to a weathered barn. The road leads into the old canal town of Seneca where a sixty-five-foot-tall, 70,000-bushel grain elevator built in 1861 sits on the empty I&M's north bank. Originally the elevator was fitted with spouts through which grain could be loaded directly onto boats headed for Chicago. In the canal's heyday, such elevators appeared all along its length. This battered survivor is still in use, leased to a farmer for storage. The canal, however, is just a grassy ditch.

Go north on Route 170, Seneca's main street, to US 6, then west (left) to Marseilles, which has a well-worn but cheerful center of taverns, antique shops, a bowling alley, and stores. From Illini State Park, just across the river, you can see its shinier side of modern riverside homes. You might also spot barges passing through the locks of the Illinois River.

Return to US 6 and continue west to Route 71. Turn south (left) into Ottawa, where an aqueduct once carried the canal over the Fox River. Past Oogies Drive-in (where carhop service is still available) you'll come to Washington Park, Ottawa's town square and site of the first Lincoln-Douglas Debate on August 21, 1858. Those were the days when politics ranked as entertainment: the debate drew 10,000 people. Facing the square is the Reddick Mansion, a swanky three-story red stone building trimmed in limestone. It was one of the most expensive Italianate homes in the Midwest in the mid-1800s, built by real estate magnate William Reddick.

Leave the town center via Ottawa Avenue, past the cemetery where the founder of the Boy Scouts of America, Ottawa publisher William D. Boyce, is buried. Ottawa Avenue becomes Dee Bennett Road and passes by industrial plants, a seedy factory town, silica quarries, and a modern nursing home before reaching Buffalo Rock State Park. The park surrounds a bluff inhabited by Native Americans when explorers Louis Jolliet and Father Jacques Marquette paddled by in

1673. A trail leads to great vistas of the river. From a wooden platform visible from the parking area, near the paddock for a small bison herd, there is an instructive view over the remains of strip mines and a multimillion-dollar rehabilitation project gone awry: five massive modern earth sculptures—of a water bug, a turtle, a catfish, a frog, and a snake—in the style of ancient mound building were carved out by bulldozers in 1984 and 1985. You won't be able to tell what they are unless you hire an airplane, but critics loved them. Now the mounds have degenerated into eroded weed patches because the soil is too poor to grow grass—unless the state finds the funds for massive doses of fertilizer and lime, and other maintenance. If signs warn you not to walk among the mounds, heed them: bullets have sometimes flown over the sculptures from a shooting range across the highway. The state filed a complaint against the range, but the case was still pending at the time of this writing.

Farther along Dee Bennett Road, the U.S. Army Corps of Engineers set up the Illinois Waterway Visitors Center at a lock and dam—enormous structures when compared to the lilliputian I&M locks. Exhibits point out again the strategic importance of the I&M Canal to Illinois history: the state's population grew by more than one million during the twenty years following its completion, primarily along the canal corridor. But the view across the river will divert your attention from the displays: the steep sandstone bluffs of Starved Rock State Park rise abruptly, and we'll visit there shortly. Barges are likely to be churning by in the foreground, especially in winter. During the coldest months, the fast-flowing Illinois River remains navigable after the Mississippi freezes over, so many barges move to this route.

Continue to the end of Dee Bennett Road and turn north (right) on Route 178 into Utica. A canal-era warehouse has been turned into the La Salle County Historical Museum, one of those all-purpose repositories. It shows off a carriage that transported Abraham Lincoln, plus relics from the Black Hawk War and pioneer days. The museum has restored a stone blacksmith shop where you may find a third-generation smithy clanking red-hot metal into shape. The blacksmith is located just behind Duffy's Tavern, the "Cheers" of Utica. If you're in town on the right weekend in October, you can dig into some burgoo, a pioneer dish bubbling in huge iron kettles over open fires.

Return south on Route 178 and cross the river to Starved Rock State Park, one of the most popular in Illinois. The rustic Great Room of its lodge, constructed of stone and timbers by the Depression-era Civilian Conservation Corps, has a massive eye-stopping fireplace. It's a great place to curl up after a hike in the forest.

Legend has it that around 1769 Illiniwek Indians took refuge atop the park's 125-foot sandstone butte, trapped there by Ottawa-Potawatomi tribes until they died of starvation. More than fifteen miles of trails wind through eighteen canyons beneath a canopy forest. Waterfalls rush down the sides; pools form from water that oozes through the porous rock. Ferns and liverworts cling to the canyon walls, and harebells, reindeer lichen, yews, and mountain holly—all survivors of the Ice Age—grow in the cool, moist habitat. If you can't get enough, more steep sandstone canyons with hiking trails have been etched into the less-traveled Matthiessen State Park near Starved Rock. (To reach Matthiessen, head south on Route 178.)

Our final destination town is La Salle. To get there, go south from Starved Rock on Route 178 to Route 71. Turn west (right) to Route 351, which leads across the Illinois River and into La Salle. Just over the bridge, turn left to the I&M Canal's Lock #14, restored to its original nineteenth-century appearance. To the west you'll find what remains of the final lock and a basin where cargos were transferred to steamboats for shipment downriver. The narrow canal joins the wide river, still a busy marine highway.

Our route ends here. From Route 351 you can reach I-80 to the north or I-39 via US 6.

In the Area

Heritage Corridor Visitors Bureau, 81 N. Chicago Street, Joliet, IL 60431: 815- 727-2323 or 800-926-2262

Lemont Chamber of Commerce: 708-257-5997

Lemont Historical Society Museum: 708-257-2972

Cookie Jar Museum (Lemont): 708-257-5012

Nick's Tavern (Lemont): 708-257-6564

Will County Historical Society Illinois & Michigan Canal Museum and Pioneer Settlement (Lockport): 815-838-5080

Public Landing Restaurant (Lockport): 815-838-6500

Weits Café (Morris): 815-942-0686

Rockwell Inn (Morris): 815-942-6224

I & M Canal State Trail
Channahon Access: 815-467-4271
Gebhard Woods: 815-942-9669
Buffalo Rock: 815-433-2220

Goose Lake Prairie State Natural Area: 815-942-2899

Illini State Park (Marseilles): 815-795-2448

Reddick Mansion (Ottawa): 815-433-0084

U.S. Army Corps of Engineers Illinois Waterway Visitors Center (Ottawa): 815-667-4054

La Salle County Historical Society Museum (Utica):
815-667-4861

Starved Rock State Park (Utica): 815-667-4726; lodge
reservations: 815-667-4211

Matthiessen State Park (Utica): 815-667-4868

5 ~

Railroads, Rivers, & Utopia

From Chicago: Take I-80 west from Chicago for about 120 miles to exit 33, Route 78, and drive south to Johnson Sauk Trail State Recreation Area.

From Davenport, Iowa: Take I-80 east to Route 78. This trip runs from the park south and west through Galesburg, then farther west to the Mississippi River, where it turns north toward the Quad Cities (Moline and Rock Island, Illinois, and Davenport and Bettendorf, Iowa).

Highlights: *Kewanee, the "Hog Capital of the World"; Bishop Hill Heritage Museum, Jenny Lind Chapel, Galesburg Railroad Museum; Carl Sandburg and Wyatt Earp birthplaces; restored remnants of utopian societies; Johnson Sauk Trail State Recreation Area, Big River State Forest, old-fashioned Mississippi River towns.*

Hogs are shedding their Porky Pig image these days thanks to a slick advertising campaign touting today's slimmer, trimmer swine as the source of "the other white meat." This trip begins in hog country where you can see these lard-free porkers for yourself.

Head south from I-80 on Route 78, where the Henry County seat of Kewanee proclaims itself the "Hog Capital of the World." The title dates to 1948 when the county indeed led the world in pig production. Representative Frank Johnson's resolution that year in the Illinois general assembly to designate Kewanee as Hog Capital was greeted by legislative hog calls and pig squeals. He put the pork-barrel politicians to shame, however, by telling how hogs fed Illinois pioneers and played a vital role in the state's economy.

Our first stop, a little north of Kewanee, is the 400-acre Johnson Sauk Trail State Recreation Area. Set on the old Sauk Indian trail, the park is the site of a magnificent round barn. Eighty-five feet high and eighty feet in diameter, it's thought to be one of the largest in the country. It was built in 1909 as part of a summer getaway spot by Dr. Laurence P. Ryan, a brain surgeon and plastic-surgery pioneer who headed Chicago's Loyola University Medical School. He had all the lumber shipped in by train and wagon, then soaked in water and shaped to the proper curve. The design included all sorts of labor-saving ideas, such as a drainage system into underground "slurries" beneath the barn from which liquid manure could be pumped out to fertilize the fields. The doctor stocked

A round barn . . . with "no corners where the devil might hide"

the barn with imported black angus show cattle. Most of the other "round barns" in Illinois aren't fully round but have vertical siding or are more octagonal. Such barns were originally built by religious groups who wanted "no corners in which the devil could hide."

South of the Johnson park on Route 78, signs point you east (left) toward Francis Park and an unusual home that is open for tours in the warm-weather months. It's named for Fred Francis (1856–1926), an eccentric mathematician and inventor who constructed this ungainly one-story brick house with air conditioning, running water, a water purification system, doors that open automatically, and windows that disappear—all powered *without* electricity. Almost everything remains in working condition.

To reach Kewanee, head south from Francis Park to US Route 34, then southwest; or backtrack to Route 78 and go south to the town. Kewanee takes its title of Hog Capital of the World seriously even though the county now ranks only sixth in the nation in hog production. Each Labor Day weekend, Kewanee plunges whole hog into a Hog Capital festival: the town decorates itself in a hog motif, and residents and visitors pig down 30,000 or more pork chops. There are stuffed pigs as carnival prizes, hog stampede races, and hog souvenirs. Hog-calling and kiss-a-pig contests occur in alternate years as well as numerous nonpig events.

Kewanee also boasts a pair of one-and-only sites: Good's Furniture is the only combined furniture store, German Rathskeller, bed and breakfast, and hair salon in the world. A block away is a savings bank with otters swimming in its lobby.

Phil Good's great-grandfather started Good's Furniture store in 1895. Phil's wife Mary began working at the store as a high-school cheerleader saving for college. She stars in the store's TV commercials and has become one of the best-known faces in northern Illinois; people think of her as the sweet-tempered girl next door. The Goods opened a luxurious three-room bed and breakfast in one corner of the store to house customers from far-flung points, but now even honeymooners reserve space. The charming Rathskeller, operated by Mary's sister Kathy, was started to feed hungry shoppers (incidentally, Kathy makes her own breads, pastries, and pies the old-fashioned way, i.e., with lard in the piecrust). When Kathy's husband wanted to try a hairstyling business, Good's offered him the space. The furniture galleries cover 65,000 square feet in two buildings connected by a skywalk, with atriums and a glass elevator.

Inside Union Federal Savings at Tremont and First streets, two male river otters romp and roll in a sunken pool outfitted with waterfalls, slides, and rocks. The playful critters had always fascinated bank president Robert Hansen—so much so that when the building was scheduled for expansion, he decided to incorporate an otter exhibit. Hansen spent months researching zoo architecture and otter behavior. School groups (and grown-ups) visit the otters to giggle at their frolics and learn why they're endangered in Illinois.

Exit Kewanee on Route 78/US 34, and continue on US 34. The rolling countryside is ideal for combining hogs with corn, their main food. The thinner layer of soil on the hillsides doesn't hold up if crops are planted year after year, so a cornfield one season becomes a hog pasture the next. These pastures are dappled with little houses—the size of a St. Bernard's doghouse. Each sow claims one and builds a nest inside where she gives birth to her piglets. I saw one such youngster tearing across a field toward the rest of the porkers with half a dozen feeder calves galloping after it. Was the little guy leading a charge, or were the calves chasing him away?

You'll see more pigs, more corn, then Galva, an agricultural town settled by Swedes in 1854. Galva is the source of Jacobsen's Swedish-style rusks (toasted breads), created according to a recipe Mrs. Minerva Jacobsen perfected in her home kitchen more than sixty years ago; you can find them in area grocery stores. (Though the rusks are made in Galva, Jacobsen's also operates a bakery at 208 W. Fifth Street in Kewanee.) Cross the train tracks and continue on US 34, turning north (right) at a sign pointing toward Bishop Hill.

In 1846, a religious zealot named Erik Jansson broke with the state church of Sweden and led his followers to an agrarian communal "utopia on the prairie." That first winter, the handful of settlers lived in caves hollowed out along a ravine; ninety-six died. But more colonists arrived, and the pious, hardworking Swedes built twenty large commercial buildings and farmed 12,000 acres. By the 1850s, Bishop Hill residents were dwelling in comfortable apartment buildings while other pioneers were still living in primitive log cabins.

Like most utopian schemes, however, this one went awry. Jansson was murdered in 1850, and though the village thrived economically, the commune was dissolved in 1861 because of the Civil War and charges of financial mismanagement. The community's original buildings have been restored to their 1860s appearance with the help of the Janssonists' descendants. They are scattered on wide, shaded lots around a block-square park.

The Bishop Hill Heritage Museum in the Steeple Building includes more than ninety works by settler Olof Krans, house painter turned artist, portraying the hardships and triumphs of those early days. Krans is now recognized as one of America's foremost folk artists.

Bishop Hill, with only 160 residents, today has restaurants, craft and gift shops, antique stores, and bed and breakfasts—all with a Swedish theme. Many jams, jellies, and regional craft items are for sale. I bought some things at the

Bishop Hill Colony Store, the center of community life for more than a hundred years, with the assistance of a blond-haired preschooler. Sitting on the counter, she slowly rang up my purchase on an old-fashioned cash register, with just a little prompting from her mother.

You might want to plan a visit to Bishop Hill for Jord-bruksdagarna (Agricultural Days) in late September to see old-time harvest and craft demonstrations. Or come during Julmarknad, the annual Christmas market in late November and early December, for Swedish foods, baked goods, and gifts.

Return to US 34, and follow it through the little farm towns of Altona and Oneida to Galesburg, our next major stop.

Travelers keen to learn more about the area's Swedish heritage will enjoy a side trip to Andover, about twenty miles northwest of Bishop Hill. To get there from Bishop Hill, return to US 34 and take it to Route 17 heading west. Turn north (right) onto Route 82, then west (left) on Route 81 to reach the village. Andover was founded in 1835 by pioneers from New England, who were joined by Swedish settlers after 1840. The Jenny Lind Chapel here is named for the singer known as the "Swedish nightingale," who made a sizable contribution to its construction in the early 1850s; the mother church of the Augustana Lutheran Synod, the chapel houses a small museum. Andover's second Lutheran church, built in the 1860s, still stands, as do the Swedish Methodist Church, the first in the country (1855), and a number of homes with Swedish connections. The fastest way from Andover to Gales-burg is to head west on Route 81, then south on I-74 or US 150.

Galesburg is the "big city" on this route. It was founded on an idealistic scheme by a New York Presbyterian preacher named George Washington Gale, who was alarmed at the lack of education and religion on the frontier. He and his followers bought and settled land here and opened Knox Manual Labor College, where students were to pay for their instruction by doing manual labor. The plan quickly failed and the school became Knox College, the first college in Ilinois to provide higher education for women and to graduate a black. Its handsome Old Main building was the site of a Lincoln-Douglas debate in 1858. (Descendants of one of Galesburg's original families, the Ferrises, introduced popcorn to England and invented the Ferris wheel.)

Railroads—the arteries that opened the Illinois prairies to agriculture and commerce—arrived in 1854. Galesburg remains a railroad town where engines moan through the night. The Railroad Museum, open during the summer, has restored a 1930 Hudson-type 4-6-4 passenger engine so powerful that engineers never opened its throttle all the way; they could feel the locomotive lifting off the tracks before reaching full speed. The museum is located south of Main Street on Seminary Street next to a restored train station with gleaming oak ceilings, wall panels, and waiting room benches. During Galesburg's Railroad Days, held annually around the beginning of June, the town is aquiver with street fairs, railroad memorabilia, and gandy dancer olympics—a spike-driving competition among railroad employees.

South of the tracks at 313 E. Third Street is the simple three-room cottage, now a museum, that was the 1878 birthplace of Carl Sandburg, author, poet, socialist, and product of this railroad town. Sandburg's father, a Swedish immigrant, was a blacksmith for the Chicago, Burlington & Quincy Railroad. Sandburg never lost touch with his working-class roots, which are evident in everything from the braided rugs to the plain furnishings in this tiny home. Behind the home, his ashes are buried beneath a rock bearing his words, "For it could be a place to come and remember."

Head west from Galesburg on US 34 to Monmouth, where the nation's first sorority, Pi Beta Phi, was formed at Monmouth College. In 1848, Monmouth was the birthplace of Wyatt Earp, who became the U.S. marshal in Tombstone, Arizona, and with his brothers and Doc Holiday outshot the bad guys at the O.K. Corral. Several times a year, the shootout is reenacted in Monmouth. The Earp home is located at 406 S. Third Street, and some Earp family members are buried at the pioneer cemetery on N. Sixth Street, where the last burials took place in 1857.

Continue west on US 34. You'll soon zip downhill onto flat Mississippi River bottomlands. Turn north (right) on Route 164. Just beyond the hamlet of Gladstone, you'll cross Henderson Creek and spot a red covered bridge in a grove of trees on your right. It was built for $2,125 in 1866 from oak beams held together by wooden pegs. Anybody who drove more than a dozen horses, mules, or cattle across at one time or led a beast faster than a walk was fined $5.00. The bridge washed away in 1982 but was retrieved, rebuilt, and sited several feet higher than before so it would stay put.

You're now entering a territory named Oquawkiek ("yellow banks") by the Sac and Fox Indians for the sandy banks on the Mississippi's eastern shore. Warm-weather months see fish frys and boating events all along this stretch of river.

Oquawka is the first of a series of river towns—funky amalgams of homes, empty storefronts, small businesses, and vacant lots sitting side by side in sleepy downtowns. Clusters of restaurants and taverns often cater to boaters as well as landlubber locals. (Adventurous eaters might try Kathy's Fine Food Restaurant in Oquawka, which serves savory Chinese dishes.)

Oquawka was originally a small trading post, and the county historical society is restoring one of its earliest homes, the 1833 Augustus Phelps house. Augustus chose a fine spot with wonderful river views from atop one of those yellow bluffs. As in any number of river towns along here, Oquawkans once manufactured pearl buttons from mussel shells.

Near the town's water tower is the grave of Norma Jean, a thirty-year-old elephant felled by lightning on July 17, 1972. The 6,500-pound Norma Jean, the performing pachyderm of the Clark & Walters Circus, was buried on the spot—rolled into her twelve-foot grave with a heavy chain and a tractor. Her trainer, Larry "Possum Red" Harsh, fared better: he was thrown thirty feet by the bolt but survived. Norma Jean's headstone, topped by the sculpture of an elephant with its trunk pointing toward heaven, contains a bulletin board with clippings about her death.

Go east out of Oquawka on Route 164, soon turning north on a county road toward Keithsburg. You'll pass fresh fish stands, farms irrigating the sandy soil, and the Sin City Resort. Hmmm. . . . Beyond Delabar State Park is the 3,000-acre Big River State Forest, a remnant of a prairie woodland border community where amateur botanists can hunt the rare large-flowered penstemon and Patterson's bindweed. You'll discover a lovely picnic spot on wooded bluffs above the Mississippi backwaters and a trail where you can still see the wagon ruts of the 2,000 men who forged north through here on their way to the Black Hawk War. If you're along this route in winter, keep your eye out for bald eagles.

Keithsburg has put up plaques marking its earliest buildings, including the 1835 Robert Keith house on Washington Street. You can rent the tiny 1853 Ellett House by the day or week. Down at the river on Main Street, the Lighthouse Tap draws folks from miles around to its Sunday breakfast buffet.

Up the street at Cheryl's Dolls, Cheryl Reeder creates exquisite porcelain dolls. Cheryl and her husband, Rex McIntire, have restored a number of the town's nineteenth-century historical buildings.

Continue north on the county road to Route 17, where you turn west (left). You'll see Sloan's produce market, a summer shopping stop, just before you turn south (another left) into New Boston, dead-ending at a former ferry landing on the Mississippi. The most poignant of New Boston's shuttered downtown buildings is the Abe Lincoln Hotel, where a ground-floor shop once sold "old stuff and funny little things." A spanking white Methodist church sits proudly in the village, along with the New Boston Museum (in an 1856 home) and a restored Victorian mansion or two.

Backtrack north out of New Boston on Route 17, but when Route 17 turns east, you don't. Instead, head onto County Road A, marked as the Great River Road, which travels west briefly before turning north toward Route 92. The Mississippi River floodplain widens here into rich farmlands. You'll notice signs pointing toward river access points popular with hunters, fishermen, and boaters. The farm just before Route 92—where you'd expect to see more hogs or Holsteins—is raising llamas, emus, sheep, and goats instead. Cute-but-serious signs warn you to beware of the spitting llamas.

The route's final leg travels east (right) on Route 92 to Illinois City and turns left at a Great River Road sign onto West 238th Street at Massey's Hillbilly Corner, then rolls along a hilly stretch with long views over the Mississippi valley. Andalusia was the most noted river crossing north of St. Louis in the 1830s, when ferries carried thousands of settlers to Iowa and beyond. Like other towns along the Mississippi,

Andalusia was a pearl button manufacturing center. Now it's the final river town before you reach the interstate highways ringing the Quad Cities.

In the Quad Cities, you'll find a host of hotels, motels, restaurants, and sightseeing stops, from riverboat casinos to Civil War sites and art museums.

In the Area

All numbers are within area code 309.

Western Illinois Tourism Council, 107 E. Carroll Street, Macomb, IL 61455: 837-7460 or 800-232-3889

Henry County Tourism Council: 927-3367

Yellowbanks Heritage Association (Keithsburg): 374-2659

Kewanee Chamber of Commerce: 852-2175

Johnson Sauk Trail State Recreation Area (Kewanee): 853-5589

Good's Furniture (Kewanee): 852-5656

Jacobsen's Home Bakery (Galva): 932-2560

Bishops Hill Heritage State Historic Site and Museum: 927-3899

Galesburg Area Convention and Visitors Bureau: 343-1194

Galesburg Railroad Museum: 342-9400

Carl Sandburg State Historic Site (Galesburg): 342-2361

Monmouth Chamber of Commerce: 734-3181

Ellett House (Keithsburg): 582-3343 or 800-346-5323

Cheryl's Dolls (Keithsburg): 374-2479

Keithsburg Museum: 374-2659

Big River State Forest (Keithsburg): 374-2496

Quad Cities Convention and Visitors Bureau: 800-747-7800

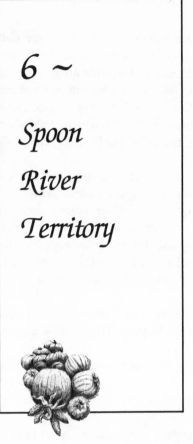

6 ~

Spoon

River

Territory

How to get there: Our trip begins in Peoria, 170 miles southwest of Chicago. We start on I-474 and make a loop through the region south and west of the city.

Highlights: *Wildlife Prairie Park, Banner Marsh Fish and Wildlife Area, Rice Lake Fish and Wildlife Area, and Jubilee College State Park; Dickson Mounds Museum; Spoon River valley towns.*

"Will it play in Peoria?" That was the question worried vaudeville performers asked themselves around the turn of the century. Peoria was known as the toughest town on the circuit, so if an act was a hit there, it figured to be a hit anywhere.

Peoria, now the second largest metropolitan area in Illinois, grew up as a brawny river port and wealthy industrial center split between hard-driving, hard-drinking neighborhoods and bluff-top boulevards lined with stately mansions. You can still "play" here aboard a riverboat casino or among Peoria's museums, historic homes, arboretums, and beautiful shady streets. But our route leaves the city to savor old-time river communities that once were steamboat stops and fishing ports, floodplain marshes and wildlife areas, a site of ancient Indian settlements, and sleepy Spoon River farm towns made famous by Edgar Lee Masters's 1915 *Spoon River Anthology*. It's a particularly lovely trip in fall when gold and red trees decorate the river bluffs and gently rolling hills.

Industrious settlers plowed Illinois prairies, drained wetlands, and chopped forests to create productive farms and industries. Another consequence of their labors was the extinction of bison, bears, wolves, and other animals that were shot as pests or whose habitats were destroyed in Illinois. The route starts with a look at some of these species at Wildlife Prairie Park on a country road outside Peoria.

Take I-474 to Route 116 west, then turn north on Taylor Road at signs directing you to the park. The wildlife lives in large enclosed spaces on natural terrain among lakes and wooded ravines of reclaimed strip mines and adjacent pastures. Cougars and black bears forage in the undergrowth; bison, elk, and white-tailed deer graze the lush grasses. Waterfowl and sandhill cranes frequent ponds and streams. Many of the bridges and habitats were built by hand to protect the natural foliage, and you'll see recycled bricks, timbers, and telephone poles used in construction of the visitors center and other buildings. You might pick up some recycling ideas you can use at home.

Tucked among the animal areas and nature trails are a pioneer schoolhouse, chapel, log cabin, and barn with animals early settlers raised—and you can pet. A railroad chugs around the grounds where you'll also find a restaurant and snack shop. You can spend a night in the wild, too, staying at the park in a cabin or one of several cabooses with bunk beds.

Return to I-474 and head south and east, exiting south along the Illinois River on US 24 through Bartonville's industrial and business section. You soon reach the countryside where patches of wildflowers and redbud trees color the bluffs in spring.

US 24's four lanes are reduced to two just before Banner Marsh Fish and Wildlife Area. Within ten minutes of entering this 4,500-acre reserve, I spotted muskrats, grebes, coots, a great blue heron, several kinds of ducks, and trees felled by beavers. (You'll also spot lots of mosquitoes during warm weather, so come prepared.) Protected by a levee, surface mining created 457 bodies of water on this floodplain, interspersed with farm fields and grasslands. Hunters and fishermen love the place, but it's also great for hiking and birding.

Still on US 24, pass through Banner, a cluster of cottages and trailers with simple motels and taverns catering to hunters and fishermen. You'll spot little Walnut Cemetery at the bottom of the bluffs and more drained bottomlands planted in crops. At Rice Lake State Fish and Wildlife Area there's a shaded campground and concession stand. The 5,700-acre reserve is managed as nesting and feeding habitat for waterfowl and migrating shorebirds. Each June, the lakes are drained and the mud flats seeded with food plants. The best birding is in early fall for those willing to trek the lakes' levees.

A few miles after Rice Lake, keep your eye out for a faded sign steering you left along zigzag Liverpool Road to Pace's Riverview Inn. Like the highway sign, Liverpool is faded, though it was once an important depot for steamboats carrying goods to Canton, Lewistown, and other inland communities. At the turn of the century, more than 2,000 commercial fishermen worked the length of the Illinois River harvesting nearly 25 million pounds of catfish, carp, buffalo, and bass. According to Bill Pace, a former coal miner who now owns the

Riverview Inn, Liverpool was a major fishery during that period. The bustling town had four hotels, ice houses, and shops in addition to its fisheries. It drew hunters, too—including Chicago gangster Al Capone and his pals.

By the mid-1950s, thanks to industrial pollutants and raw sewage washed downstream via the Chicago Sanitary & Ship Canal, plus silt from eroding farm fields along the banks, the Illinois River was almost dead. Efforts have been made to clean up the river, but all that's left of Liverpool's downtown is a post office, a tavern, and the Riverview Inn, whose walls are lined with photos from the old days. The restaurant serves as many as 400 people a day on weekends, temporarily quadrupling the town's current population.

Continue on US 24. Little America, a river town where tidy and tumbledown houses mingle, has a small antiques mall; a handsome horse resides in the paddock next door. Three miles later, turn south (left) on Route 78/97, which travels down the bluffs onto what was once a lake bed. You're passing through the 13,000-acre Norris Farm, where the thick black soil is called "riverbottom gumbo." Owned by the Morton Salt family, the farm was created by draining a lake and swamps. You'll see a Norris feedlot on your left.

Cross the Spoon River and turn east (left) on Route 97/US 136, which soon carries you over the Illinois River to Havana. Rusty barges tied up along the river hint at the river traffic of the mid-1800s when hundreds of steamboats carried grain and produce from Havana. Like Liverpool, Havana became a major fishing port where daily catches of 100,000 pounds were not uncommon. The town is quieter now, and some of its downtown is shuttered, but it still depends on the river.

Along Havana's shady streets—some paved in brick—you'll discover the pleasant riverside McNutt Guest House (409 W. Main Street) and a few delightful shops like Granny

Annie's antiques on the Mason County courthouse square. Three good places to try some Illinois cooking are Kenny's Café on Main Street, noted for home-cooked meals, Poor Richard's, also in downtown Havana, and the Depot in the former railroad depot (naturally).

Because of its sandy soil, Mason County irrigates more than any other part of the state. This porous soil is ideal for growing watermelons, cantaloupes, sweet corn, pumpkins, and other produce. Head any direction into the county, and you'll find seasonal farm stands with fresh-picked vegetables and melons.

Return across the Illinois River from Havana and turn north (right) on Route 78/97. Then turn west (left) to Dickson Mounds Museum, set on a tall bluff. Here the skeletons of 237 Indians buried a thousand years ago were displayed as archaeologists had found them, until 1992 when they were reburied at the insistence of Native Americans. Even without the burial display, the museum is worth visiting. The displays explore 12,000 years of Indian life found in the remains of campsites, villages, and burial mounds, and trace the change from loose-knit hunter-gatherer groups to controlled, structured societies concentrated in fortified towns.

Retrace your route a short distance to a sign pointing west (right) toward Waterford Church and Orchard Hill Farm. You're entering the heart of Spoon River country immortalized in Edgar Lee Masters's *Spoon River Anthology*. Waterford's first permanent white settler was John Eveland, who arrived in 1820 with his wife and twelve children in a cottonwood pirogue.

The village of Waterford was formed here but was abandoned by the late 1800s. Several nineteenth-century buildings remain or have been moved here from other parts of the county. Scattered in grassy fields, they seem more poignant than if they had been clumped together as an outdoor museum. The 1839 school, also used as a church, is the only remaining building from the original village. The tiny Plank Road Toll Booth nearby used to be on the Lewistown Road. Around a corner down the road you'll see the 1892 Waterford Town Hall, which serves as the township polling place, and the 1890 Waterford Union Church, also still in use.

A little farther along the main road, Orchard Hill Farm's owners grow popcorn, pumpkins, squash, Indian corn, red raspberries, asparagus, peaches, apricots, and forty varieties of apples. It's worth a stop in the fall just to crunch into one of their caramel apples.

Continue to Lewistown, turning north (right) on Main Street. When Edgar Lee Masters was eleven, his family moved to Lewistown from Petersburg, into a modest frame house at the southeast corner of Main and D streets; the house is still there, but is not open to the public. His *Spoon River Anthology*, published in 1915, is a series of poetic monologues by 244 inhabitants who tell their own interwoven stories from

In Illinois farm country

beyond the grave. Some of the characters were recognizable figures in and around Lewistown, and the portraits Masters painted weren't pretty; he ripped the lid off the respectable, idyllic image of small-town life.

As you drive up Main Street, you can easily imagine a turn-of-the-century Lewistown. The 1882 Rasmussen Blacksmith Shop was operated by the family until 1969, when it became a museum. The 1850 Spoon River Hotel now has a video arcade on its ground floor. Across Lincoln Avenue from the hotel is the white frame New England-style Presbyterian Church from 1856, and on the other side of Main Street is Fulton County's fourth courthouse. Its predecessor, built of brick in 1838, had a portico with four stone columns where Abraham Lincoln stood in 1858 to deliver a ringing speech. In 1894, an arsonist set fire to it, providing fodder for Masters's poem "Silas Dement":

> . . . the glorious bon-fire, growing hotter,
> Higher and brighter, till the walls fell in
> And the limestone columns where Lincoln stood
> Crashed like trees when the woodman fells them.

Two of the columns were re-erected in the Oak Hill Cemetery in front of the Civil War monument.

Further north at 1127 Main Street is the 1850 home of Major Newton Walker (not open to the public), who hosted Lincoln several times. Walker planned and built the third courthouse, and Masters mentions him in the opening poem of the anthology. Walker died in 1899 at age 96.

Across the street from the Walker home, Oak Hill Cemetery spreads across a knoll. This is the setting for Masters's masterpiece. On Edgar Lee Masters Day in late May or early June, local people dress in period costumes and read from the anthology while standing beside the graves of the people who inspired the individual poems. Tombs related to the *Spoon*

River Anthology have numbered white markers beside them corresponding to a list you can purchase with the book at the Lewistown Chamber of Commerce (119 S. Adams Street) or at the Rasmussen Blacksmith Shop Museum.

Lewistown also is a starting point each October for the Spoon River Valley Scenic Drive Fall Festival, a route through spiffied-up rural communities offering homemade food, crafts, farm demonstrations, and other events. You can make the drive, minus the special events, any time of year and still find it scenic and relaxing.

Go north out of Lewistown on Main Street (Route 97/ 100), and stay on Route 97 to Cuba. You'll dip into a shallow valley and up again onto the flat farmlands. Cuba, supposedly named by someone who moved here from Havana, Illinois, was the site of Fulton County's first strip mines in the early 1920s. As a result of the former mines, the whole region is pocked by lakes, some of which have been stocked for fishing.

Route 97 jogs east through tiny Fiatt, then north again at a former gas station and café. At Main and Market streets in Fairview, the two-story Dutch Reformed Church, with green-shuttered windows on both floors, was built in 1837 and is the oldest of its denomination west of the Alleghenies. Fairview's downtown has a little country grocery, a beauty shop, a café, and a greenhouse.

Continue north on Route 97 to Route 116 and turn east (right), passing through more strip-mining territory to Farmington. Downtown, Zellmer's Main Street Dinner Theater packs 'em in from Peoria and surrounding territories for rousing musical hits. The cast can even perform "Singin' in the Rain"—in the rain. That's because the old red brick silent movie theater later became a Moose Lodge, and what's now the stage area was its kitchen, with excellent drains in the floor. So theater-owner Don Zellmer and his troupe can tap-dance beneath the sprinklers.

Go on through town on Route 116 to its intersection with Route 78. There you'll find Shad Hill, a dark brown two-story barnlike structure filled with folk arts, handmade crafts, antiques, a fine arts gallery, and a restaurant. The building was constructed of weathered wood gathered from more than twenty barns, and incorporates a frosted etched window from the old Farmington post office and other salvaged beauties. Sponsored by the Two Rivers Arts Council, Shad Hill serves as a shop, studio, and performance area for 150 or more folk artists from the region. You might arrive when one of them is weaving wheat into animals and angels or stitching squares into place on a quilt.

Travel north on Route 78 to Elmwood, the birthplace of Lorado Taft (1860–1936), whose native and transitional sculptures injected a breath of midwestern fresh air into a European-dominated art scene. In the town square is Taft's memorial to his parents, a bronze statue of a young settler with his wife, child, dog, and gun. A museum devoted to the sculptor occupies a small white house at 302 N. Magnolia Street. On the main highway, you can't miss the tidy two-story Neptune Fire Company No. 1, red brick with white trim and a bell tower; it now houses city offices. All it needs to be a Norman Rockwell vignette is a Dalmatian out front.

Continue on Route 78 to US 150 and turn east (right) through Brimfield to Jubilee College State Park and Historic Site. The 3,500-acre park, on rolling grounds along Jubilee Creek, surrounds the site of Jubilee College. The school was opened by the first Episcopal bishop of Illinois, Philander Chase, who had already had a long career as priest, missionary, pioneer bishop of Ohio, and founder of Kenyon College. In 1835, at the age of 60, Chase toured England soliciting funds to found the Illinois seminary, then moved his family to a log cabin in Peoria County.

The cornerstone of a chapel, the college's first building, was laid on April 3, 1839, "a day fine, the sky serene, and just enough wind to remind us of the breath of God," Chase wrote. The institution owned 4,000 acres and operated farms and mills with the hope of being economically self-sufficient. After Chase's death in 1852, though, the school dwindled financially until its doors closed in 1862. The chapel and an attached dormitory, constructed of yellow native stone, remain on a knoll above the creek. An odd picture on the rugged frontier, these Gothic-style buildings are more easily envisioned in a cultured New England village of the mid-1800s. In late June each year, a rollicking fifteenth-century-style Olde English Faire is held here.

Our route ends here at Jubilee College. If you continue on US 150 to Kickapoo, you'll find an entrance to I-74, which will whisk you back to Peoria.

In the Area

All numbers are within area code 309.

Western Illinois Tourism Council, 107 E. Carroll Street, Macomb, IL 61455: 837-7460 or 800-232-3889

Fulton County Tourism Council: 547-3234

Peoria Area Convention and Visitors Bureau: 676-0303 or 800-433-7399

Havana Chamber of Commerce: 543-3528

Lewistown Chamber of Commerce: 547-4300

Wildlife Prairie Park (Peoria): 676-0988

Banner Marsh State Fish and Wildlife Area (Canton): 647-9184

Rice Lake State Fish and Wildlife Area (Canton): 647-9184

McNutt Guest House (Havana): 543-3295

Dickson Mounds Museum (Lewistown): 547-3721

Orchard Hill Farm (Lewistown): 547-3221

Spoon River Scenic Drive (Ellisville): 293-2143

Rasmussen Blacksmith Shop (Lewistown): 547-7274

Zellmer's Main Street Dinner Theater (Farmington): 245-2554

Shad Hill (Farmington): 245-4452

Lorado Taft Museum (Elmwood): 742-7791 or 742-2431

Jubilee College State Park (Brimfield): 446-3758

Jubilee College State Historic Site (Brimfield): 243-9489

Accommodations

All points on this route are within easy distance of Peoria, which offers a wide range of accommodations. You'll also find motels in Farmington, Lewistown, Canton, and Harvard, plus campsites at Canton Lake and near Lewistown and Havana.

Just north of Peoria, not far from Kickapoo and near where this route ends, are several bed and breakfasts, including Eagle's Nest Bed and Breakfast (Dunlap), 243-7376; and Old Church House Inn (Mossville), 579-2300.

7 ~

Nauvoo to Macomb

From Chicago: Take I-80 west to I-74 just east of Moline. Drive south to Galesburg, follow US 34 west to the Mississippi River, then take Route 96 south along the river to Nauvoo.

From St. Louis: Take I-61 north to Keokuk, cross the river, and take Route 96 north to Nauvoo. Or stay on I-61 to Fort Madison, cross the river, and take Route 96 *south* to Nauvoo. This trip ends at Macomb, about forty miles east of Nauvoo. (NOTE: Coming from St. Louis, the trip is faster if you follow the route *backward*— from Macomb to Nauvoo.)

Highlights: *Nauvoo's historic Mormon sites, Icarian Living History Museum, vineyards, state park, arts and crafts; beekeepers and honey products; towns of Hamilton, Warsaw, and Carthage; Cedar Glen Preserve, Earth Center for the Arts, and Argyle Lake State Park; a round barn, Western Illinois Threshers ground, Antique Gas Engine Show, Western Museum at Western Illinois University.*

Nauvoo, on a grand horseshoe bend of the Mississippi River in western Illinois, was the state's largest city in early 1845 with an estimated population of 20,000. It was the headquarters of the Church of Jesus Christ of Latter Day Saints founded by Joseph Smith fifteen years earlier. By 1847, most of its residents had departed on a westward migration after armed conflict with the region's non-Mormons.

Our route begins at the two dozen restored Mormon homes and public buildings of the mid-1800s in modern Nauvoo, plus other historic sites built by later settlers—a group of French communists called the Icarians, then German farmers and tradesmen. We'll follow a lovely stretch of the Mississippi River south to Warsaw, whose roots thread back to the War of 1812. Then it's inland through farm country to the college town of Macomb, now with the same population Nauvoo achieved in its heyday.

"I was descending the last hillside upon my journey," wrote U.S. Army Colonel Thomas L. Kane of an 1846 visit to western Illinois, "when a landscape in delightful contrast broke upon my view. Half encircled by a bend in the river, a beautiful city lay glittering in the fresh morning sun; its bright new dwellings, set in cool green gardens, ranging up around a stately dome-shaped hill, which was crowned by a noble marble edifice. . . ."

This was Nauvoo toward the end of its brief glory, when more than 2,000 neat brick and frame houses and buildings were packed along checkerboard streets. The city spread across a tongue of land poking against the Mississippi and worked its way up the river bluffs. Today, only two dozen or so of the town's original buildings are scattered like preserved bones across the flat promontory. Modern Nauvoo lies on the plains above and makes its living from tourism and agriculture.

Joseph Smith, who founded the Church of Jesus Christ of Latter Day Saints (LDS) in 1830, was driven out of Missouri with his followers. He led them to the swampy, mosquito-infested village of Commerce, Illinois, comprised of half a dozen crude buildings. Smith wrote, " . . . no more eligible place presenting itself, I considered it wisdom to make an attempt to build up a city." And that he did.

Smith changed the town's name to Nauvoo and struck a deal with the Illinois legislature to make it a city-state: Smith was to be mayor, court justice, head of the militia, and controller of all the votes. The diligent Mormons drained swamps and quickly built a thriving community that included a 165-foot-high temple on the bluffs. Converts arrived to swell the population.

The two dozen buildings remaining from early Nauvoo create a powerful image of the city at its height. Center of Nauvoo social life was the three-story Cultural Hall (now restored), scene of dances, plays, and formal meetings. The smell of gingerbread cookies wafts from the Scovall Bakery next door. The 1842 home of Jonathan Browning, inventor of the repeating rifle, contains his gun shop with a display of the firearms he designed.

You can also explore a drug store, a printing office, a blacksmith shop, a mercantile store, a tin shop, a shoemaker's shop, a brickyard, a school, a missionary training center, and a number of homes, all outfitted as they were in the early 1840s. Many feature demonstrations of pioneer crafts. In July and August, you can spend an evening at the outdoor historical musical, "City of Joseph," with a cast of more than 300.

Even when filled with tourists in midsummer, Nauvoo is more peaceful than in the fall of 1845, when it echoed with the sounds of hammers and saws as its residents built wagons and prepared to head west.

Many of the region's non-Mormons had come to hate the Latter Day Saints. Word was out that the religion permitted polygamy, and there were fears that Mormons would take over politically—especially after Smith declared himself a candidate for president in 1844. After Smith ordered the destruction of the presses of a dissenting newspaper, he, his brother Hyrum, and two other Mormon leaders were arrested and placed in the county jail at Carthage (which comes later on our route). A mob stormed the building and shot the Smith brothers to death. Brigham Young took over as leader and led the Mormons west in 1846.

By the end of that year, Nauvoo was a virtual ghost town. Only a few Mormons remained, including the family of Joseph Smith. Believing the church's leadership should be

This intriguing gunsmith shop is one of
many historic buildings remaining in Nauvoo

hereditary, they broke away to found the Reorganized Church of Jesus Christ of Latter Day Saints (RLDS). Among Nauvoo's most important sites for all Mormons are the homes and graves of Joseph Smith, his wife Emma, and brother Hyrum. The Mormon Temple was burned by arsonists in 1848, but a monument stands in the square it occupied.

The Uptown Information Center on Route 96 has a cassette tape tour of the historical sites. Both the LDS and the RLDS have visitors centers with films and audiovisual presentations about Nauvoo and Mormonism, gift shops and displays. Church members staff the meticulously restored buildings. It is an integral part of their religion to convert others, and non-Mormon visitors may find some members quite enthusiastic and time-consuming in presenting the history and philosophy of their church.

Many travelers miss Nauvoo's other historic sites, which mingle with the present-day town. The Icarian Living History Museum, in a restored 1840s home on Parley Street, presents the story of French settlers who brought their version of communism to Nauvoo in 1849. They purchased Temple Square and began a short-lived experiment in communal living that ended about 1855.

Some of the Icarian settlers remained, however, and were joined by Germans, Swiss, and others. Emile Baxter, who arrived in 1855, began vineyards now operated by his descendant, Kelly Logan. Baxter's Vineyards, the oldest winery in Illinois, is open for tours and tastings. In what is now Nauvoo State Park, which runs up the bluffs behind old Nauvoo, Lichtensteiners Alois and Margretha Rheinberger planted vines in 1851 that are still producing. Their eight-room home and the winery, as well as another wine press from a fellow settler, are maintained in the park as a museum.

By 1866, Nauvoo counted some 250 vineyards and sixty cellars, one of which is now given over to the production of tangy blue cheese, for sale in local supermarkets and shops.

This French wine-and-cheese heritage has been celebrated since the 1930s during the September Grape Festival's Wedding of the Wine and Cheese pageant.

Old-fashioned crafts and skills are exhibited uptown. At Nauvoo Mill and Bakery, millers use stone grinding wheels to produce wheat, corn, and other flours and meals for baking. Outstanding pieces are produced at Nauvoo Glassworks. Antique stores include Ruh's Hardware, half given over to refinished furniture and antique items.

Hotel Nauvoo, a dolled-up 1840 residence, serves the best food in town in seven dining rooms. A popular eatery for locals is Dottie's Red Front, a tavern that packs people in for a Friday night catfish fry.

Nauvoo has a campground plus a number of small motels and bed and breakfasts. A favorite is Mississippi Memories just south of town on Route 96. This contemporary home, with two wide decks overlooking the river, is owned by Marge and Dean Starr, who operate a large grain and livestock farm nearby. The strip of river from Nauvoo to Warsaw is prime geode-hunting territory, and you might discover some on the Starrs' property. Geodes, round rocks with crystal-filled cavities, are found along streambeds, particularly after gully-washer rainfalls. You must ask permission of the landowner before rock-hunting on private property.

Along the twelve miles from Nauvoo to Hamilton, Route 96 hugs the river, rising over occasional wooded hills for long views across the water. You'll find picnic spots all along where you can stop to drop a fishing line, watch the barge and pleasure-boat traffic, or spot waterfowl. Wood ducks nest in a protected area just south of Nauvoo.

Keep your eye peeled for farm stands selling vegetables, jams, and jellies in addition to fresh strawberries, grapes, and apples. A few antique shops and campgrounds as well as old houses made of soft yellow limestone are tucked among the gentle bluffs.

Hamilton begins close to the river and continues up-hill onto flat crop-growing fields. Its business district retains the small-town components of barber shop, tavern, café, insurance office, and furniture store—even in the face of strong competition across the Mississippi in the Iowa city of Keokuk.

Turn west toward Keokuk on US 136, and just before the bridge, pull in at Dadant & Sons' long, three-story stone building. Dadant is a buzzword in Hamilton: for more than 130 years, the Dadant family has been devoted to the business of beekeeping—from hives to honey and the bees themselves. In 1863, Charles d'Adant emigrated from France to start a vineyard. He kept honeybees for pollination and sold their output. Today his great-grandson Tim Dadant (the family name was Americanized) is president of the company.

"The building we're in was originally a tire manufacturing company," Dadant told me. "My grandfather purchased it and we've been here ever since." The company publishes a beekeeping journal, how-to books, and honey cookbooks. Small display rooms show off twisted, honeycomb, and other types of candles, honey cosmetics, and honey itself.

Just past the Dadant building, turn left at a sign pointing toward Warsaw. The county road rises over a wooded hill, atop which sits the Alice L. Kibbe Life Science Station. It is used for research and education at the 1,205-acre Cedar Glen preserve, held jointly by The Nature Conservancy, the Illinois Department of Conservation, and Western Illinois University. The preserve includes Mississippi shoreline and islands, limestone bluffs, upland oak-hickory forests, maple-sycamore glens, cottonwood floodplains, glacial sand hills, and prairies. You can pick up a map at the station to explore twenty miles of trails that offer great birdwatching. Fourteen species endangered or threatened in Illinois have been sighted here, including the little blue heron and the northern harrier.

The preserve's most spectacular visitors are the 400 or more bald eagles that find the Mississippi lock and dam just north of the Keokuk bridge a fine winter fishing site. From November 1 to March 1, the preserve is closed to protect the eagles from disturbance. But they can be easily seen from Montebello Park, just north of US 136 in Hamilton, or from the site of Fort Edwards in Warsaw. January and February are the best eagle-viewing months, and the birds are most active from sunrise until about 10:00 A.M. on clear days.

The road winds on through forested landscape into Warsaw, which grew on the site of forts built during the War of 1812. Major (later president) Zachary Taylor oversaw construction of the first fort in 1814, but it was soon abandoned. A second, Fort Edwards, went up in 1817. Its site is on a bluff over the river backed by shady residental streets and a square graced with a miniature Statue of Liberty.

Laid out in 1834, Warsaw rapidly became a lively river port with two breweries, a distillery, three flour mills, a woolen mill, an iron foundry, a plow factory, three opera houses, a packet boat company, and other businesses. One of its early nicknames was "Spunky Point," reflected in the ballads of Warsaw native John Hay, President Abraham Lincoln's private secretary and later secretary of state under presidents William McKinley and Theodore Roosevelt.

Two of the five men tried and aquitted for the murder of Mormon leader Joseph Smith and his brother Hyrum were Warsaw natives. One was Thomas Sharp, editor and publisher of the *Warsaw Signal*, just down Main Street from the historical society's museum. Members of the mob that killed the Smith brothers gathered after the shootings at the former Fleming's Tavern at Main and Second streets. Much of Warsaw is on the National Register of Historic Places, but like many once-thriving river towns, it now looks a bit time-worn. However, some of the original mansions have been beautifully restored to their old-fashioned dignity.

Return to US 136 and go east (right) through Hamilton. A sign points north (left) toward the Western Illinois Threshers grounds, and if you're here the first weekend in August, head that way. The grounds feature a one-room schoolhouse, a log cabin, and an old train depot. The twenty-five-year-old threshing event was the brainchild of Fred Bucker.

"We'd collected many old tractors, cars, trucks, fire trucks, and other things and had been going to other shows," Bucker said. "I thought, 'Shoot, let's show the young folks around *here* how things used to be done,' and it progressed from there." Each year, the show features seventy-five to a hundred tractors of a single make, such as John Deere or J.I. Case. Also part of the show are about 150 antique tractors of all makes, plus other farm equipment, antique cars and trucks, and small gas engines and motors "like the kind that ran your washing machine when they first went from doing it all by hand," Bucker added. Some ten to fifteen thousand people come to watch yesteryear's farming techniques.

If you're hungry in Hamilton, stop at Fort Worth Barbecue, whose owner is a W.C. Fields look-alike who dishes up luscious turkey, pork, and beef sandwiches from outdoor cookers. You'll find it along US 136 as you head east out of town.

US 136 pierces the flat landscape like a straight arrow, changing course a bit at Elvaston to reach Carthage, a rural town that has been the Hancock County seat since 1831. Carthage is the site of the old stone jail where Joseph and Hyrum Smith were lodged in an upstairs bedroom—for their own protection—when the mob killed them. The Latter Day Saints restored the jail and living quarters and added a visitors center next door decorated with paintings depicting Mormon history. You can watch an orientation movie and have a free tour of the jail.

The 1908 county courthouse several blocks away is one of the handsomest in Illinois. Its interior includes six marble staircases decorated in brass, wrought iron, and wood; mosaic tile floors; carved, painted, and molded walls; domes over the rotunda, courtroom, and main stairwell lined with leaded stained glass; and the original chandeliers and lighting fixtures. The wide lawn is the scene of a farmers market, Octoberfest, and other community activities.

Continue on US 136 toward Macomb. Flat farm fields are broken by branches of the narrow LeMoine River, which adds the texture of low hills and wooded plots to the landscape. Colchester is announced by a feed and grain elevator and a blue water tower, but few businesses have survived. Turn north (left) at signs for Argyle Lake State Park.

Just before the park, you'll spot the beehive kilns of a defunct brick and tile factory that's being resurrected as the Brickyard Campus of the Maryland-based Earth Center for the Arts. When the brickyard closed in the 1960s, its grounds became an informal dump—until stained-glass artist Dev Genovese decided in 1991 to buy it and convert it to an environmentally conscious arts center. The former factory building has become a glass and pottery studio with equipment made from recycled materials. As money and manpower become available, the machine shop will become a gallery and reception hall; five kilns will be used as workshop studios and galleries.

Across from the entrance to Argyle Lake is the true-round Kleinkopf barn, built in 1914 and a popular subject for artists and photographers. Quite a contrast is the tumble-down round barn you'll find just a quarter mile northwest. The Kleinkopf building is one of more than three dozen historic wooden barns on a self-guided auto tour of McDonough County available from the tourist office in Macomb. The tour is a good way to edge into Colchester and Macomb by rural roads. Along the zigzag routes, you'll learn about agricultural architecture from barn styles such as the locally-unique cross-gable variety and those with hip- and half-pitch roofs. The decorative woodwork on the stick-style, basilica-type Everly barn and buildings makes them look like museum pieces.

In Argyle Lake State Park, a man-made lake occupies Argyle Hollow, which was on the stage route between Galena and Beardstown. Five miles of moderate to very difficult hiking trails wind around the lake through virgin forests. You might sight a beaver dam, wildflowers, and some of the 200 bird species recorded in the area. The park is the site of old-fashioned wheat threshing, hay baling, sawmilling, quilting, and other crafts at its Antique Gas Engine Show each Labor Day weekend.

Return to US 136 and continue to Macomb, the McDonough County seat that ends our route. The city is the home of Western Illinois University, where the Western Museum displays Civil War and Abraham Lincoln artifacts and documents. Macomb centers on the bustling square surrounding its county courthouse, a striking red brick and cream Italianate building from 1872—with a clock that still works! You'll find a choice of accommodations, restaurants, antique and secondhand shops, a farmers market, and a host of events that may tempt you to stay a while.

In the Area

Western Illinois Tourism Council, 107 E. Carroll Street, Macomb, IL 61455: 309-837-7460 or 800-232-3889

Nauvoo Chamber of Commerce, P.O. Box 41, Nauvoo, IL 62354: 217-453-6648

Carthage Tourism Center: 217-357-3119

Warsaw Information Center: 217-256-4235

Macomb Area Convention and Visitors Bureau:
309-833-1315

Church of Jesus Christ of Latter Day Saints Visitors Center
(Nauvoo): 217-453-2237

Reorganized Church of Jesus Christ of Latter Day Saints
Visitors Center (Nauvoo): 217-453-2246

Icarian Living History Museum (Nauvoo): 217-453-2437

Baxter's Vineyards (Nauvoo): 217-453-2528

Nauvoo State Park: 217-453-2512

Hotel Nauvoo: 217-453-2211

Dottie's Red Front (Nauvoo): 217-453-2284

Mississippi Memories Bed and Breakfast (Nauvoo):
217-453-2771

Dadant & Sons (Hamilton): 217-847-3324

Alice L. Kibbe Life Science Station (Cedar Glen Preserve,
Warsaw): 217-256-4519

Carthage County Jail Latter Day Saints Visitors Center
(Carthage): 217-453-2237

Brickyard Campus, Earth Center for the Arts (Colchester):
309-776-3444

Argyle Lake State Park (Colchester): 309-776-3422

Western Museum (Macomb): 309-298-1727

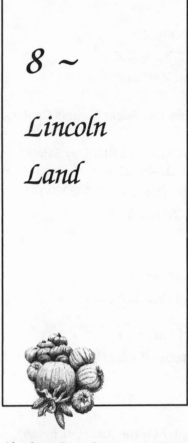

8 ~

Lincoln Land

From Chicago: Take I-55 for about 200 miles southwest.

From St. Louis: Take I-55 northeast for about 90 miles. This trip is based in the Springfield area.

Highlights: *Living history at New Salem State Historic Site; Lincoln's home, law offices, and the Old State Capitol—complete with an original copy of the Gettysburg Address—and much more in Springfield; other historical and recreational sites in Salisbury, Petersburg, Lincoln, Clinton, and Decatur.*

Abraham Lincoln was an Illinoisan through and through—although he was born in Kentucky in 1809, reached his twenty-first birthday in Indiana, and attained greatness in Washington, D.C.

"Perhaps this is so because Lincoln grew with his state," wrote Governor Henry Horner in the vintage 1939 *WPA Guide to Illinois.* "Lincoln and Illinois had met in youth and grown together; the people of the prairies had taken this young backwoodsman to their hearts and made him one of them, and he repaid them with trust and affection and an implicit recognition of their common destiny."

After his nomination for the presidency in 1860, Lincoln told the *Chicago Press & Tribune* that his early years in Kentucky and Indiana could be condensed into a single sentence from Gray's Elegy: "The short and simple annals of the poor." In Illinois, he achieved his ambitions, turning himself from a barely educated laborer into a prominent attorney and political leader.

The Lincoln Land route reaches some of the most important scenes in Lincoln's Illinois years—settings where you can gain an understanding of this complex man who led our country through the dark days of the Civil War. As Lincoln comes to life in his old haunts, you'll discover his very human characteristics of "skepticism, anxieties, self-doubts, contradictions, loves, laughs, enlightenments, failures and triumphs," in the words of Stephen B. Oates in his outstanding Lincoln biography, *Malice Toward None*. These qualities are the reason so many of us can identify with him 130 years after his death.

This chapter differs from most in *Country Roads of Illinois* in that you'll travel more or less chronologically in Lincoln's life rather than from place to place. All the sites are within easy driving distance of Springfield, where Lincoln spent most of his adulthood and where he is buried.

Early in 1830, twenty-one-year-old Abraham Lincoln moved from Indiana to Illinois with his father Thomas, stepmother Sarah, and her children. John Hanks, a cousin, had settled on the bluffs of the Sangamon River ten miles southeast of the fledgling town of Decatur and wrote glowing reports. After the Lincoln clan arrived, the men raised a log cabin and planted crops at a site now marked by a plaque at Lincoln Trail Homestead State Park south of US 36/I-72 on County Road 27, about 35 miles east of Springfield.

Over the summer, Abraham and John split several thousand rails for farmers in the area. (Thirty years later when the state Republican convention met in Decatur, John hauled in a banner tied between two of the old rails to support Lincoln's candidacy for president, thus creating his image as the home-spun "rail splitter." Delegates endorsed Lincoln as a favorite son candidate for president. Hanks later sold old rails from Macon County farms as souvenirs for $1.00 each.)

Lincoln had accumulated only a year or so of formal education, but he'd read a history of his country and hung out at the log courthouses near his Indiana home. He'd pored over the *Revised Statutes of Indiana*, and studied the Declaration of Independence and U.S. Constitution. So it was no surprise that the young man made his first political speech on a fall day in 1830. He arrived at Decatur's public square in time to hear part of an oration against the Whigs, the predecessor of the Republican Party. Lincoln is said to have mounted a stump to laud the Whig candidate in response. A statue of a barefoot Lincoln with one foot on a stump stands in the downtown square where the event occurred.

Later that autumn, everyone on the Lincoln farm fell sick with ague, a malarial fever marked by high temperatures and the shakes. In December, a blizzard raged through; then a freezing downpour added a layer of ice to the high drifts. Livestock froze to death or were eaten by wolves. For about nine weeks, the temperature stayed at twelve degrees below zero. In March 1831 the snow melted and rivers flooded the prairie. Lincoln's parents had had enough. They moved south with Sarah's children to another homestead in Coles County.

That spring, Abraham, with his cousin John Hanks and stepbrother John Johnston, hired out to speculator Denton Offutt to accompany him on a flatboat carrying produce from Springfield to New Orleans. The young men headed off to meet Offutt and make their fortune. On the way, they stopped in New Salem, where Offutt arranged to open a store on his return. New Salem was a brawny, two-year-old pioneer village then, with two saloons, a tavern, and a pair of general stores. Its small population ranged from drunken riffraff to respectable, educated folks. The town served as the backdrop for Lincoln's young manhood.

To reach New Salem State Historic Site, a reconstructed village on the bluffs above the Sangamon River, travel west from Springfield on Route 97, which turns north through Salisbury.

At the historic site, more than two dozen log and clapboard buildings come to life as living-history craftsmen and interpretive guides recreate the Lincoln years. The smell of

Lincoln log cabin

baking bread and simmering stew drifts from a cabin kitchen. The blacksmith's hammer clangs on a red-hot horseshoe. A farmer leads a team of oxen up the lane.

The visitors center houses a museum and theater where The Great American People Show presents Lincoln-related and other productions during summer months (you'll need to order tickets in advance). Special events throughout the year have included quilt shows, storytelling, and music festivals. The surrounding park includes a restaurant, campground, bookstore, and paddle wheel excursion boat that's a replica of the *Talisman*, the only steamboat to struggle successfully up the Sangamon as far as New Salem.

In this thriving new village, twenty-two-year-old Abraham was on his own for the first time, tall and gangling, with big ears, a hawk face, a high-pitched voice, and hair that wouldn't stay put. He had little formal education, but he was a superb athlete—a fast runner and strong wrestler with muscles like wire. Just back from New Orleans, he worked as a clerk in Denton Offutt's store, reconstructed on the bluffs overlooking the Sangamon. It neighbors Bill Clary's store, also rebuilt, where the brawling, hard-drinking Clary Grove boys hung out. Lincoln outwrestled and outfoxed the Clary gang and gained their lifelong respect and friendship.

But he wanted more than good-time friends. He wanted to "get hold of something that was knotty." So young Lincoln joined the debating society and did well—to the surprise of the local schoolmaster (whose schoolhouse is on the site)—and embarked on a rigid self-improvement program, studying grammar, mathematics, poetry, and politics.

At New Salem, you'll find the places where Lincoln worked as shop owner, surveyor, and postmaster, swapping stories and news. In 1832, the young Lincoln ran for the state legislature and lost (though he polled 227 of 300 votes in the New Salem precinct). Two years later, at age twenty-five, he ran again and won. By then, he'd earned his nickname of Honest Abe, a straightforward man who paid his debts.

As a legislator, Lincoln became intrigued by the law and borrowed law books. He'd study late at night at Henry Onstot's cooper shop, the only original building left at New Salem. In warm weather, he liked to lie on his back reading, with his long legs propped up against a tree trunk. In 1836 Lincoln was licensed to practice law, and the following year, he decided his future lay in Springfield, the state capital.

By 1840, New Salem was a ghost town. Many of its residents had moved two miles north to the busy trading center of Petersburg, and you can follow them, traveling north again on Route 97.

Petersburg stretches along the Sangamon valley and up its bluffs. Lincoln had ties with the town while living in New Salem and Springfield. The village had been laid out in 1833 by George Warburton and Peter Lukins, friends of Lincoln. It didn't grow fast enough for them, so the partners sold it in 1836 to John Taylor and Hezekiah King, who hired Lincoln to resurvey their purchase.

Petersburg became the seat of Menard County, part of the Eighth Judicial Circuit that Lincoln rode each spring and fall from 1839 to 1847 to argue cases that ranged across the legal spectrum. (Documents relating to Lincoln's law practice are displayed on the second floor of the county courthouse on Petersburg's town square.)

The grave of auburn-haired Ann Rutledge, Lincoln's legendary sweetheart, lies in the Oakland Cemetery on the southwest edge of Petersburg, moved here from the Concord Cemetery near New Salem. Ann's father had operated the tavern at New Salem and founded the debating society that Lincoln joined. Ann was already engaged when she met Lincoln, who became a fast family friend. In 1835, her death from "brain fever" plunged Lincoln into depression, an affliction that plagued him throughout his life.

Lincoln, Illinois, northeast of Springfield on I-55, is the only city named for the sixteenth president during his lifetime with his consent. [If you decide to go there from Petersburg, take Route 123 to Route 29, where you turn north (left). Then go east (right) on Route 10.] In 1853, developers hired Lincoln to prepare documents for a town they were plotting immediately north of Postville and they named it in his honor. On August 27, 1853, after the first lots were sold, crowds cheered for a "christening," so Lincoln broke open a watermelon and used its juice to officially name the new town. The christening site, near the present Amtrak railway station at Sangamon Street and Broadway, is marked by a monument shaped like an ear-to-ear watermelon slice.

The village of Postville served as Logan County seat from 1837 until it was moved to Mt. Pulaski ten years later; later it was absorbed by Lincoln. Postville's original two-story, walnut-sided courthouse, a stop on the judicial circuit that Lincoln rode, was purchased by Henry Ford, who shipped it to his Greenfield Village Museum in Dearborn, Michigan. A reproduction stands in Postville Park at Fifth and Washington streets in Lincoln.

Mt. Pulaski, site of one of only two county courthouses in Lincoln's judicial circuit still standing, sits northeast of Springfield on Route 54, at the intersection with Route 121 leading from Lincoln. The striking Greek Revival courthouse stands atop the highest point in town and is outfitted in furniture and books of the mid- to late-1800s.

Northeast of Mt. Pulaski on Route 54 lies Clinton, the home of Lincoln's legal associate Clifton H. Moore, whose Victorian mansion, The Homestead, is now a museum. On July 27, 1858, Stephen A. Douglas presented a three-hour campaign speech in the town square here. In his response that evening, Lincoln said the now-familiar words: "You can fool some of the people all of the time, and all of the people some of the time, but you can't fool all the people all of the time." A statue of Lincoln marks the spot.

Lincoln was no fool when he decided to move to Springfield in the spring of 1837, shortly after the Illinois supreme court enrolled his name as a lawyer. It was here that Lincoln won his reputation as an accomplished lawyer and politician, and where he married Mary Ann Todd, member of a distinguished Kentucky family.

To meet the mature Lincoln and his family, visit their home on the corner of a four-square-block area restored to the board sidewalks and gas streetlights of the 1850s. It is steps away from the National Park Service Visitor Center at 427 S. Seventh Street, where you can pick up a free ticket for a guided tour through the home, browse a bookshop, and view programs and exhibits on Lincoln's years in Springfield.

Once you step inside Lincoln's Quaker-brown frame house, it's easy to imagine the Lincoln family at home on a typical evening—perhaps in early September of 1859, a little more than a year before his election to the presidency of a divided nation. Lincoln's black stovepipe hat hangs in the alcove beneath the front staircase. He's in the sitting room considering an invitation to speak at a Republican rally in Columbus, Ohio, later in the month. Six-year-old Tad leans against his father's lanky legs, filling papa in on his day. Willie, age nine, is out back doing chores. Mary Todd Lincoln supervises dinner preparations in the kitchen, telling the maid how much she misses sixteen-year-old Robert, who left home the week before to enter Phillips Exeter Academy in New Hampshire.

By 1859, Lincoln was a well-to-do attorney and politician, making $5,000 a year when the average income was around $400. He and Mary were remarkably permissive parents, and the Lincoln boys were considered holy terrors by their neighbors and relatives.

Lincoln's law offices from 1843 to 1852, which he shared first with partner Stephen Logan and then with William Herndon, are at Sixth and Adams streets, five blocks from his home and across from the Old State Capitol. It was a convenient building to have offices in since the state's only federal court and a post office were downstairs. A guided tour shows that Lincoln wasn't much at keeping records; he kept one envelope marked, "If you can't find it anywhere else, look in here."

In the 1840s and 1850s, the Greek Revival-style State Capitol was the scene of concerts, dances, and political rallies. In 1840, Lincoln was beginning his fourth and final term in the state legislature; he and his Whig colleagues had done some heavy politicking to get the seat of government moved here from Vandalia. During the next twenty years, Lincoln's political fortunes were molded at the Old State Capitol. Here he researched election returns, used the libraries to prepare cases, swapped stories with clerks, and pleaded at least 243 cases before the supreme court.

Most days you have the choice of taking a guided tour or walking through the Old State Capitol on your own. On Fridays and Saturdays, however, because of the number of visitors, guided tours are required—and you'll be accompanied by costumed actors portraying characters from the 1850s. You'll see the spot where Lincoln launched his unsuccessful 1858 campaign for the U.S. Senate against Stephen Douglas with the words: "A house divided against itself cannot stand. I believe this government cannot endure, permanently half slave and half free."

As president-elect, Lincoln used the governor's office as a reception room. An original copy of his Gettysburg Address, purchased by donations from Illinois schoolchildren, is in the lobby. You'll also see the spot where more than

75,000 people filed past Lincoln's open coffin following his assassination in Washington in 1865.

Whether you visit several other Lincoln sites in Springfield depends on your level of interest in the details of his life. In a moving address, President-elect Lincoln bade farewell to Springfield from the former Great Western Railroad depot on Monroe Street, which has been restored as a museum. His family pew is in the First Presbyterian Church. The home of poet Vachel Lindsay, previously owned by Lincoln's sister-in-law, was the site of his preinaugural farewell reception. And his account ledger with Springfield Fire & Marine Insurance Company is in the lobby of Marine Bank.

The Lincoln's Tomb in Oak Ridge Cemetery north of downtown should not be missed, however. Inside the 117-foot-tall monument, the remains of Mary and three of Lincoln's four sons are buried near his own red marble sarcophagus. Lincoln's body actually lies ten feet beneath the floor of the tomb in a vault constructed secretly after an attempt to steal the corpse for ransom in 1876.

Outside, rub the shiny nose on the bronze bust of Lincoln created by Mt. Rushmore sculptor Gutzon Borglum: it brings good luck.

Other Sights to See

The Lincoln Land route contains additional sightseeing stops, plus dining spots and special events. Here's a sampler:

Springfield

- State Capitol, Second and Capitol streets. Construction began in 1860, but it wasn't ready for the legislature to move in until 1877. It has been the center of state government ever since.

- Executive Mansion, Fifth and Jackson streets, is the third oldest continuously occupied governor's home in the nation. Fourteen rooms are open to the public.

- Illinois State Museum, Spring and Edwards streets, has three floors of exhibits on Native Americans, anthropology, Illinois history, fine arts, and natural history.

- Illinois Artisans Shop, Eighth and Capitol streets in the Lincoln Home National Historic Site, has prints, jewelry, ceramics, sculpture, quilts, carvings, clothes, and more created by some of the state's finest craftsmen and artists.

- Dana Thomas House, 301 E. Lawrence Street, was designed in 1902 by Frank Lloyd Wright and is the most perfectly preserved example of his early work.

- Henson Robinson Zoo, 1100 E. Lake Drive, is a small zoo with some 200 animals in gardenlike surroundings.

- Lincoln Memorial Garden and Nature Center, at 2301 E. Lake Street, was designed by landscape architect Jens Jensen to reflect the Illinois countryside of the mid-1800s. Five miles of trails.

- Maldaner's Restaurant, 222 S. Sixth Street. Springfield has many dining choices, but this spot is a personal favorite. Just around the corner from the Lincoln-Herndon law offices, it's done in old-fashioned dark wood and serves creative, tasty dishes. Downstairs is casual, upstairs is comfortably sophisticated.

- The Lincolnfest each July is mid-America's largest FREE family street festival, covering eighteen square blocks with eight stages featuring continuous entertainment and music.

- The Illinois State Fair each August features agricultural exhibits, animals, horse racing, entertainment, and constant activities.

Salisbury

- You literally can't miss folk artist George Colin's home and workshop on Route 97 between Springfield and New Salem. The yard is a kaleidoscopic jungle. This retired Pillsbury flour bagger paints anything that sits still: garbage bins, planters, chairs, ladders. Some are in blinding shades of pink and green; others, like a hip-high Holstein or Abe Lincoln mailbox, are more muted. Three-quarters of his pieces are made of recycled materials.

Petersburg

- Masters Home, Eighth and Jackson streets. *Spoon River Anthology* author Edgar Lee Masters spent his early years in this tiny white frame house.

- More than four dozen early homes and businesses are the subject of a self-guided tour available at Petersburg's Chamber of Commerce offices in the Menard County Historical Museum at Seventh and Jackson streets.

- Carmody's Clare Inn, 207 S. Twelfth Street, is a bed and breakfast in an 1874 mansion. A newcomer B&B is The Oaks, an 1875 Italianate mansion, operated in conjunction with the turn-of-the-century Smoot Hotel at Sixth and Douglas streets, where you'll find an antique ice cream parlor, lounge, restaurant, and antiques mall downstairs, and guest rooms upstairs.

Lincoln

- The Lincoln Museum at Lincoln College displays a collection of more than 2,000 volumes, manuscripts, art, and other items related to our sixteenth president.

- The Lincoln Depot Restaurant, next to the railroad tracks where Lincoln christened this community, is in the town's original train station. It is one of the places President Lincoln's funeral train stopped while returning his body from Washington to Springfield.

- Abe's Caramelcorn Shoppe, 129 N. Kickapoo Street, caters to your sweet tooth. It's in a handsome red stone building with high arched windows. Caramel corn, candy, and other items are displayed on old-fashioned wood shelves.

- September's Abraham Lincoln National Railsplitting Contest and Crafts Festival features its namesake competition plus handcrafted folk art, old steam engines, and a flea market. At August's Art and Balloon Fest, dozens of hot air balloons take to the sky while almost a hundred juried artists display their works on the ground.

Mt. Pulaski

- Pharis' Memories 'N' Meals on the square across from the old courthouse sports an old-fashioned soda fountain up front and restaurant in back.

Clinton

- The Dewitt County Museum at The Homestead, Clifton H. Moore's mansion, includes a century-old carriage barn with buggies and sleighs, a farm and railroad museum with rail memorabilia and vintage farm machinery, a covered bridge replica, and country store.

- Weldon Springs State Park, southeast of town, was a popular spot on the Chautauqua circuit; now you can camp, fish, or picnic there.

- Clinton Lake, to the east, is a 10,000-acre recreation area with marinas, swimming, hiking trails, camping, and winter sports.

Decatur

- Governor Richard J. Oglesby's 1875 Italianate mansion is open for tours once a month. Oglesby, U.S. senator and three-time governor, was a confidant of Lincoln. Three mapped-out walking tours of the neighborhood, which is richly endowed with other historic mansions and buildings, are available from the Decatur Area Convention and Visitors Bureau.
- The Rock Springs Center for Environmental Discovery, 1495 Brozio Lane, has hundreds of programs and events through the year. It's the site of the well-done Decatur Area Children's Museum, a long-grass prairie, and an 1860s prairie farm.
- Scovill Zoo, on a bluff overlooking Lake Decatur, displays 500 animals in ten acres.
- A replica of the county's first courthouse, a small log building, is in Fairview Park. Lincoln tried only one case here.
- Many country roads end at A.E. Staley Manufacturing Company and Archer Daniel Smith, two of the largest processors of corn and soybeans in the United States. The fact that Illinois is the country's number one producer of soybeans and ranks second in corn becomes quite clear when you see the row upon row of massive silos and refining plants. It's worth a drive by Staley's 400-acre plant with 151 buildings on Route 105 in the east end of town, where an average of 200,000 bushels of corn are processed each *day*. Its fourteen-story 1929 headquarters building, lighted each Christmas, is an Art Deco beauty. Unfortunately no tours are given, but

stick your head into the striking lobby if you're there during working hours. Outside the business environment, Staley is best known for hiring George Halas to organize the Decatur Staleys football team, which eventually became the Chicago Bears.

In the Area

All numbers are within area code 217.

Central Illinois Tourism Council, 629 E. Washington Street, Springfield, IL 62701: 525-7980 or 800-262-2482

Springfield Convention and Visitors Bureau: 789-2360 or 800-545-7300

Petersburg Chamber of Commerce: 632-7363

Abraham Lincoln Tourism Bureau of Logan County (Lincoln): 732-8687

Clinton Chamber of Commerce: 935-3364

Decatur Area Convention and Visitors Bureau: 423-7000

Springfield

Lincoln Home National Historic Site: 492-4150

Illinois Artisans Shop: 524-1520

Lincoln Depot (Great Western): 544-8695

Lincoln-Herndon Law Offices: 785-7289

Old State Capitol: 785-7961

Lincoln Ledger: 529-9600

Illinois State Capitol: 782-2099

Illinois State Museum: 782-7386

Illinois State Fair: 782-6661

Dana Thomas House: 800-545-7300

Governor's Mansion: 782-6450

Lincoln's Tomb: 782-2717

Henson Robinson Zoo: 529-2097

Lincoln Memorial Garden and Nature Center: 529-1111

Maldaner's Restaurant: 522-4313

Petersburg

Lincoln's New Salem State Historic Site: 632-4000

Great American People Show: 632-4000

New Salem Campground: 632-4000

Carmody's Clare Inn Bed and Breakfast: 632-2350

The Oaks Bed and Breakfast and Smoot Hotel: 632-4480

Lincoln

Postville Courthouse State Historic Site: 732-8930

Lincoln Museum, Lincoln College: 732-3155, ext. 294

Lincoln Depot Restaurant: 735-2385

Clinton Area

DeWitt County Museum, The Homestead (Clinton):
935-6066

Weldon Springs State Park (Clinton): 935-2644

Clinton Lake State Recreation Area (DeWitt): 935-8722

Decatur

Scovill Zoo: 421-7435

Governor Richard J. Oglesby Mansion: 423-7000

Rock Springs Center for Environmental Discovery: 423-4913

Decatur Area Children's Museum: 423-KIDS (-5437)

9 ~

Amish Country in the Heart of Illinois

From Chicago: Take I-57 south for 120 miles. At exit 190, follow Route 16 west to Shelbyville.

From St. Louis: Follow I-70 to exit 76 at St. Elmo. Jog east on US 40 to Route 128 north to Shelbyville. The trip ends at Arcola, just west of I-57 at exit 203.

Highlights: *Shelbyville's courthouse, historic homes, and antiques; a two-story outhouse, an excellent summer theater, an 1890s ice cream parlor, and a French restaurant in a bowling alley; Eagle Creek State Park, Chief Illini Trail, and Lincoln Log Cabin State Historic Site; Amish horse-drawn buggies, tidy businesses, tasty restaurants, and low-key entertainments.*

In 1903, Shelbyville decided to stretch its collective mind and build a Chautauqua auditorium for summertime lectures, concerts, and plays. A local machine shop owner named H.B. Trout designed a multisided building with a roof held up by beams and suspension girders instead of columns. Our route begins at this dirt-floored community center of yesteryear in quiet Forest Park on the north side of Shelbyville, which lies twenty-five to thirty miles north of I-70 and west of I-57.

Here statesman and orator William Jennings Bryan and prohibitionist Carrie Nation expounded on the issues of the day and John Phillip Sousa led his band in rousing marches.

The audience waved handkerchiefs in the air in approval—the "Chautauqua salute." Affluent folks built summer cottages around the auditorium; the less wealthy rented tents (floor boards cost extra). Today the Chautauqua auditorium echoes with family picnics and kids, in a mad game of tag, shrieking with laughter as they dart among the trees.

Shelbyville lies at the south end of Lake Shelbyville, created more than twenty years ago when the Kaskaskia River just east of town was dammed. The county courthouse on Main Street (Route 16), a brick-and-stone eyepopper, towers over the river valley and massive earthen barrier like a carefully coiffed Victorian grande dame.

On the east side of the dam, the Corps of Engineers visitors center perches above the lake. An aerial view of the twenty-mile-long waterway looks a bit like a root with a network of hairs insinuating themselves into every nook and cranny in the landscape. The lake is loaded with beaches, campsites, picnic areas, and marinas renting fishing and houseboats.

It's worth a detour to the village of Gays, eighteen miles further east of Shelbyville on Route 16. Here you'll see the only two-story outhouse in Illinois. This double-decker john—known as the "skyscrapper"—dates to the 1880s when it was the convenience center for the S.F. Gammill general store and the two apartments up above. The store is long gone, but the high-rise outhouse was saved and restored by local resident Pat Goodwin. It stands on a grassy area visible from the highway, with an American flag flying by its side. And how did it work? It was built with offset holes and a two-foot gap between the interior walls, so first-floor users were out of range when upper-level waste plummeted downward.

Back in Shelbyville, drive west on Main Street. Brick-paved Morgan Street and Broadway leading north toward Forest Park sport high-decorum houses from the Civil War era and later. At 207 Washington Street, just north of the courthouse, first owner John W. Yantis added a Romanesque tower. Inside there's a fold-down tin bathtub that operates much like a Murphy bed. The Queen-Anne Ward house on N. Fourth Street, just west of Broadway, also sprouts a tower, plus turn-of-the-century gingerbread. You can admire these homes from the outside; both are privately owned.

Turn north on Route 128 and plunge into pancake-flat farmland. It's hard to believe that only a mile or two to your right the landscape dips into the glacier-carved valley filled by the man-made Lake Shelbyville. Signs point toward access areas including Lone Point, starting place for the eleven-mile Chief Illini Trail that winds across rolling hills and open prairies with views over the lake and its wooded shoreline. The trail ends at the road into Eagle Creek State Park.

Turn east (right) off Route 128 toward Findlay. Antique hunters will find a multidealer mall in a brick building with arched arcades just south of the main road. Shortly after the railroad tracks, turn south (right) into Eagle Creek State Park. Here the Clarion Inn, one of the newest state park lodges, overlooks the lake, and is outfitted in country-style quilts, paintings, and handicrafts. The Clarion is a full-service resort offering restaurants, golf, massages, bike rentals, a pool and beach, tennis, a marina, winter sports, and sightseeing excursions.

Back on the main road, continue east across mile-long Bruce Findlay Bridge over the main channel of the long, skinny lake. As you cross low wooded hills, you'll catch glimpses of crooked fingers of water pointing up shallow ravines. At Route 32, the first stop sign, turn north (left) past more marinas, lake access points, and nature centers and into the central square of Sullivan.

Sullivan got its start at a mosquito-breeding intersection of prairie and stream named Asa's Point after frontier hunter Asa "Dollarhide" Rice. Like many pioneer towns, its first business was a saloon, with stores, smithies, hotels, and more saloons to follow. An infamous event occurred here in the 1858 U.S. Senate race between Abraham Lincoln and Stephen A. Douglas.

By coincidence, the two candidates arrived the same day, drawing crowds into town. After a morning of parades and hoopla, Douglas began a two-hour speech. The local *Express* reported that a little after 2:00 P.M., "as the Judge was making a point on Mr. Lincoln, which struck terror to their hearts, the abolition part of the audience hurried off . . . with full band playing and all the discordant noise that they could muster. . . ." Lincoln's supporters thereupon unveiled an enormous 24-by-64-foot wagon pulled by thrity-six yoke of oxen. A hundred or so of Lincoln's followers, including a band, clambered aboard. The procession went partway around the square then turned and plowed straight through the Douglas gathering. "In a few minutes the confusion was general, coats were drawn, clubs flourished in the air and everything seemed favorable to a general melee," said the *Express*. F.M. Green, who had created an antislavery display on the Lincoln wagon, was cracked in the head by a flying brick.

Richard M. Nixon's appearance at a buffalo barbecue here during his 1960 campaign for president against John F. Kennedy was mighty bland in comparison. That turned out to be the town's last buffalo barbecue, but something equally exciting was under way: Sullivan was building up steam as a theater town.

The Little Theater on the Square, the only professional equity summer-stock house in central Illinois, was founded in 1957 by twenty-one-year-old Guy S. Little, Jr. The young man had been intent on a stage career since he'd first seen a live production at age five. By age six he'd started his own mari-onette theater and at fifteen started acting in a New England summer-stock theater. He returned to his hometown after graduate school, leased a local movie house that was on the skids, and started producing musical comedies and dramas. When Little moved to Milwaukee as an artistic director and producer twenty-two years later, the Little Theater became a nonprofit operation and continues to stage musical comedies and children's plays.

Eventually, Little returned to Sullivan and this time converted the Queen Anne farmhouse built by his grandfather just southeast of town into the antique-filled Little House on the Prairie bed and breakfast. "I have lived and worked in New York, Miami, Milwaukee, Phoenix, Los Angeles and other places," Little told me, "and I choose to live here. It's a comfortable, wonderful place."

Sullivan has created a Sidewalk of the Stars that fans around the square from the theater past a bakery, a clothing shop, a furniture store, an antique firearms emporium, and other businesses. Granite markers embedded in the concrete salute the stars who have played here—June Lockhart, James Gavin, Betty Grable, Tab Hunter, and June Allyson among them. Their photos line the walls of Jibby's restaurant, around the corner on Main Street, which dubs itself the "Sardi's of Sullivan."

Leave Sullivan on Route 121 and travel east for about three miles to the Illinois Masonic Home, a handsome red brick building constructed in 1908 with other units added later. You'll discover a quirky little museum inside displaying some 10,000 seashells. Along with these denizens of the deep, the museum shows off antique tools, kitchen implements, and clocks, old dolls, miniature animals—including a frog licking an ice cream cone—and a pair of stuffed lizards. A. Lincoln Ward and Mrs. Cora A. Ward collected all the knickknacks and donated them to the home. If the museum isn't "officially" open when you arrive, don't despair: one of the residents will gladly take you in and flip on the lights.

Your reward for viewing all this is in the basement of the nearby Collins Building: a Gay Nineties-style ice cream parlor.

Take your cone out by a pond on the grounds and you're sure to attract some of the llamas, potbellied Vietnamese pigs, pygmy and angora goats, Sicilian donkeys, and other animals living there.

At the Masonic Home, a blacktopped road leads north from Route 121 into the simpler way of life and slower pace of a century ago. In the farm country around Arthur live about 3,400 Amish—members of a Mennonite sect who shun electricity, automobiles, telephones, store-bought clothes, and other materialistic trappings. Be aware that they do not wish to have their photographs taken except from a distance and in public places.

A roadside sign alerts motorists: "Warning—Buggies Next 12 Miles." The horse-drawn vehicles travel the highways

A patient Amish horse and buggy

and country lanes at ten or twelve miles per hour—maybe fifteen if a teenager is driving. At twilight, the black buggies can be particularly difficult to spot on the road ahead.

However, it is easy to distinguish an Amish farm after dusk. Its windows are lighted by the soft glow of lanterns rather than the glare of electric bulbs and a large-screen TV. During the day, you'll note that the roadside chain of utility poles does not sprout lines onto Amish farms. Horses can be seen grazing in paddocks or pulling plows.

A farm wife wearing a bonnet and an apron over a home-made, plain-colored dress might be hauling a load of laundry to hang on the line. Or she may be working in a huge vegetable garden out back that helps feed a large family with few expenses for anything beyond salt, sugar, and other staples. You might pass a group of men, dressed in drop-front pants with black suspenders. Those who are clean-shaven are single; married men wear a full beard without a mustache. They'll probably be speaking a dialect of German, though they also know English.

Near the intersection with the road east (right) to Cadwell is the Cadwell Harness Shop. Farming a small parcel with draft horses doesn't bring in much money, so a hundred or more Amish farmers and their wives have opened businesses like this one on their property, employing many young people who can no longer afford to buy farms because of sky-rocketing land prices.

Continue north on the blacktop road to Route 133 and turn east (right) into Arthur, the center of the country's fifth largest Amish community. On the way, you'll pass several more Amish businesses: a quilt and craft shop, a cabinet maker, a printer, and a canvas shop. Much of downtown Arthur is given over to dining spots and stores catering to tourists—restaurants specializing in Amish-style dishes like shoofly pie and gift shops selling Amish-made items. Near the parking lots on Progress Street you'll find hitch racks for the Amish buggies, with roofs to shelter the horses from the sun or rain.

Stop in the tourist office at Vine and Progress streets for a map of country businesses in the Arthur area. Staff can advise you about which ones to visit. None of these businesses is open on Sunday and some are open only on certain days. At these small shops you'll see firsthand how the Amish have adapted country skills to modern demands. They're building furniture, clocks, cabinets, and lamps, and creating quilts, candy, and foods.

From Yoder's Candy Kitchen in the basement of a farmhouse, a heavenly smell of cinnamon and chocolate wafts up the stairs. Baggies of chocolate crèmes, peanut brittle, red cinnamon bits, and a host of other varieties are displayed on practical metal shelves. A smiling young woman wearing a bonnet and apron patiently waited for us to make our choices (not an easy task!).

Down narrow lanes a half mile away, the Otto sisters operate a shop specializing in vinyl products, quilts, and crafts next door to their farmhouse. One of the sisters stitched a vinyl purse on a treadle sewing machine while she minded the shop. Many of the handsome handmade quilts were in traditional patterns such as the log cabin, the Arabian star, and the double wedding ring. At another farm, we stepped onto the back porch of the "grandpa house," a smaller home for the retired generation built next to the main farmhouse, to buy homemade apple and pumpkin butter from a wizened, gray-haired man with an Abe Lincoln beard.

Through a plate glass window at Das Schlacht Haus, a butcher shop, we watched half a dozen young men and women carving beef in spotless surroundings. The shop sells whole-hog and Italian sausages as well as other meats and chicken, and, like other profit-conscious companies, has diversified into spices, candy, homemade noodles, barbecue sauce, and other items.

You may want to time your visit to Arthur for August's Mennonite Relief Sale, a two-day auction of Amish crafts and products as well as Third World imports. The sale supports the free services the Mennonites provide in fifty countries. Or you might come during Arthur's Cheese Festival over Labor Day weekend. Now drawing more than 30,000 visitors, the event began as an open house at Arthur Cheese Company, owned by the Kondrup family of Danish cheesemakers. The company has plenty of its Swiss, Colby, Monterey Jack, and other cheeses on hand and creates a 300-foot-long submarine sandwich for the festival. No longer confined to the cheese company itself, the festival now spreads into the rest of town with stands selling crafts, foods, and baked goods, a flea market, and Amish buggy rides.

From Arthur, travel east on Route 133 through Chesterville, passing more tidy farms and country businesses. Just before Arcola, a sign points right toward an old-fashioned theme park called Rockome Gardens. More than fifty years ago, Mr. and Mrs. Arthur Martin used rocks and concrete to build fences, gates, and displays, including a heart with an arrow through it. In 1958, they sold their spread to Elvan Yoder, who turned it into a tourist attraction that is open from late April through October. Yoder added ten or more shops in a pioneer village, a quilt show and dozens of other events, a restaurant and an ice cream parlor, plus a petting zoo, a tree house, horse-powered rides, and other low-key family entertainment.

The town of Arcola was on the northern border of the broom-corn belt where farmers grew a finer-leafed type of corn used to make brooms. Three companies still make brooms, including Thomas Monohan's near the train tracks, but the corn leaves must now be imported. A restored train depot near Monohan's houses Arcola's tourist office and a small museum devoted to antique brushes and brooms. The day I visited, a jolly lady showed us the displays brush by brush. The town's annual Broom Corn Festival, which includes a sweeping contest, draws more than 50,000 visitors each September.

Arcola's small downtown benefits from tourists traveling to nearby Amish country. The Dutch Kitchen serves up fluffy four-inch-high biscuits with luscious apple butter placed on mats quoting Amish sayings translated from their German dialect: "Don't eat yourself full. There's more back yet." Or, "Eat your mouth empty before you say."

Shops all over town sell Raggedy Ann and Andy dolls. Johnny Gruelle, the artist who created the red-haired raga-muffins, grew up in Arcola, which now honors him at a down-home festival featuring a parade of kids dressed up like the imaginary urchins.

Be sure to stick your head into the Arcola Pharmacy to see its soda-fountain headquarters of the Arcola Coffee Club, begun forty years ago. Each of the 167 members has a cup with his name on it displayed behind the counter, and you'll almost always find a member there sipping a cup of java and chatting with the waitress.

Arcola's most novel attraction, however, is America's only French restaurant in a bowling alley. Chef Jean-Louis Ledent and his wife Yvette own the French Embassy Bowling Restaurant, on the corner of Routes 133 and 45 beneath tall grain silos. The couple moved to Champagne from Liege, Belgium, in 1987 and bought the bowling alley from a Belgian colleague a couple of years later. While the bowling alley snack bar serves traditional hot dogs and fries, the restaurant menu is totally French. It offers sautéed lamb with garlic, white Bordeaux and artichoke hearts, baked quail with onions, bacon, and juniper berries, and other tasty entrées. If you want to try their bouillabaisse, the Mediterranean fish soup, you have to order it a week in advance.

The route ends here, with French escargot served to the sound of bowling-alley strikes. I-57 is just east of town, providing an easy route to other parts of Illinois.

Heading South?

Abraham Lincoln's father and stepmother, Thomas and Sarah Bush Lincoln, lived their last years and were buried just south of Charleston, which lies south of Arcola on I-57, then east on Route 16. The Lincoln family moved to a farm near Decatur in 1830, but after a miserable winter spent in a crude cabin, they decided to return to Indiana. (Abe, then twenty-two, set off to Springfield on a moneymaking scheme with his cousin John Hanks and stepbrother John Johnston.) The Lincolns stopped in Coles County to visit relatives and decided to stay, eventually settling on the farm that is now Lincoln Log Cabin State Historic Site.

To get to the historic site, go south from Charleston on E Street, which becomes University Drive. You first reach the home of Reuben Moore, who married Abraham Lincoln's stepsister Matilda Johnston Hall. Sarah Lincoln was staying with Matilda in early 1861 when the newly elected president arrived there on his last stop before leaving for his inauguration. It was the last time Sarah saw him alive.

While Abraham was there, he and Sarah visited the grave of Thomas in Shiloh Cemetery south and east of the Moore home. In 1869, Sarah was buried by Thomas's side.

A half mile south of the turnoff to Shiloh Cemetery, the Lincoln Log Cabin State Historic Site includes an accurate replica of the last home of Thomas and Sarah Bush Lincoln. During summer months, the home and surrounding farm become a living history museum in which volunteers assume the roles of the Lincoln family and their neighbors. The upper-middle-class farm of Stephen Sargent, a contemporary of the Lincolns, is also in the park.

The majority of Lincoln-related sites in Illinois are visited in chapter 8.

In the Area

All numbers are within area code 217.

Central Illinois Tourism Council, 629 E. Washington Street, Springfield, IL 62701: 525-7980 or 800-262-2482

Shelby County Office of Tourism: 774-2244 or 800-874-3529 This office has information on additional sightseeing and shopping opportunities, events, campsites and recreational activities around Lake Shelbyville, motels and bed and breakfasts, including the Shelby Inn, whose office and shop are in the restored 1905 Tallman house with a pergola, a latticed pavilion, and stained-glass windows. Lodgings there range from Victorian-style B&B rooms to reasonably-priced motel accommodations.

Champagne-Urbana Convention and Visitors Bureau: 351-4133 or 800-369-6151

Shelby Inn: 774-3991

Clarion Inn (Eagle Creek State Park, Findlay): 800-876-3245

Sullivan Area Chamber of Commerce: 728-4223

Little Theater on the Square (Sullivan,): 728-7375

Little House on the Prairie Bed and Breakfast (Sullivan): 728- 4727

Illinois Masonic Home (Sullivan): 728-4394

Arthur Amish Country Information Center: 543-2242

Arcola Chamber of Commerce: 268-4530

Rockome Gardens (Arcola): 268-4106

French Embassy Bowling Restaurant (Arcola): 268-4949

Charleston Chamber of Commerce: 345-7041

Lincoln Log Cabin State Historic Site (Lerna): 345-6489

10 ~

Alton–
Kampsville
Circle

From Springfield: Take I-55 south to Route 140 west at Hamel. Route 140 goes right into Alton.

From St. Louis: Take US 67 north across the Mississippi River to Alton.

Highlights: *The mighty Mississippi and the Illinois River; the* Alton Belle *riverboat casino, the* Belle of Grafton *excursion boat, the Brussels Ferry, and other river-going options; historical monuments, statues, and parks; Vadalabene Bikeway, farm stands and U-pick produce, and a small archaeological museum.*

The 1939 *WPA Guide to Illinois* described the "faint though unmistakable backwoods flavor" of Calhoun County, squeezed between the Illinois and Mississippi rivers north of St. Louis. Fifty years later, Calhoun retains a rural air, perhaps because it's the only Illinois county the railroads never reached. On an early spring day, when fragrant patches of white apple blossoms are beginning to form on the warm hillsides, you'll meet few cars along the county's narrow blacktopped roads even though you're only twenty-five or thirty miles as the crow flies from the urban bustle surrounding the Gateway Arch.

The oldest part of Alton sits with its back to the wall—a wall of natural limestone. The rest of the town bumps up the bluffs that mark the northern head of a vast floodplain known as American Bottom that's occupied by St. Louis and its metropolitan tentacles. Alton looks out over the Mississippi River and upstream toward its junction with the Illinois River. That's the direction we'll look, too—away from the high rises and traffic jams.

Historically, Alton worked along the riverbanks and lived on the hills. Like many historic towns, Alton's downtown grew weary, and businesses moved out to the malls. But now it's starting to come alive again as some of the nineteenth-century stores and offices along terraced streets are restored, and antique shops, secondhand bookstores, and other businesses move in. The *Alton Belle* riverboat casino docks down on the landing, not far from grain elevators where 195-foot-long barges are loaded up.

Alton was founded in 1818 and at first rivaled St. Louis as a river port. Steamboats like the *Golden Eagle* hauled freight across the river, racing back from St. Louis for more; it was first come, first served. Up on Alton's steep hills, wealthy merchants topped their tall Victorian houses with elaborate cupolas from which they could observe the riverfront bustle.

In the Alton City Cemetery at the edge of the bluffs, they erected an imposing 110-foot-high monument to outspoken abolitionist editor Elijah P. Lovejoy, killed in 1837 by a proslavery mob trying to destroy his printing press. During the Civil War, Alton housed a prisoner-of-war detention camp in what had been the first penitentiary in Illinois, which opened in 1830. Reformer Dorothea Dix had waged a campaign against the state prison's harsh, unsanitary conditions, and it was moved to Joliet in 1857. But the dirt-floored facility was reopened several years later to hold Confederate prisoners. Thousands of them died during an 1863 smallpox epidemic, and 1,354 of those who died are buried in a cemetery on Rozier Street. Only a fragment of the primitive prison is left at Broadway and Williams Street.

A monument to a famous Alton resident of this century stands on College Avenue—a life-sized bronze statue of Robert Wadlow, the "Alton Giant." Towering just a half inch short of nine feet (with a shoe size of 37AA), Wadlow is listed in the *Guiness Book of World Records* as the tallest man in recorded history. He died in 1940 at age twenty-two.

Leave Alton on Route 100 west, the Great River Road, which skirts twenty miles of steep, white limestone bluffs, rock layers tilted skyward along the Cap au Gres fault. The Vadalabene Bikeway parallels the road as far as Pere Marquette State Park, winding to hilltop viewpoints and crossing creeks and ravines on arched bridges.

Only a few miles beyond Alton, the cliff face of a former quarry bears a modern rendition of Indian paintings of the legendary Piasa bird—"the bird that eats men." Father Jacques Marquette recorded his impressions of the original paintings as he and Louis Jolliet traveled down the Mississippi in 1673:

> As we were descending the river we saw high rocks
> with hideous monsters painted on them, and upon
> which the bravest Indians dare not look. They are as
> large as a calf, with head and horns like a goat; their
> eyes red; beard like a tiger; and a face like a man's. Their
> tails are so long that they pass over their heads and
> between their forelegs, under their belly, and ending
> like a fish's tail. They are painted red, green, and black.

The Piasa bird that Father Marquette saw was blasted away during quarrying operations in 1870. The current version looks more like a dragon designed to frighten toddlers than a man-devouring bird.

As the road winds along the river, there are long views of the wooded bluffs. Just past Piasa Creek, look across the Mississippi for Our Lady of the Waters, a statue of the Virgin placed there after all of Portage-des-Sioux, Missouri, was flooded except for its Catholic church. Each July boats crowd around her feet for the Blessing of the Fleet.

In another ten miles or so, Route 100 reaches Elsah, nestled in a narrow ravine along Askew Creek. In 1847, the village was known as Jersey Landing and most of its residents chopped wood to sell to steamboats. General James Semple, a retired Illinois senator and diplomat, bought much of the land in 1853, changed the name to Elsah, and developed gristmills and a distillery. He gave a lot to anyone who would build a stone house on it. When railroads superseded steamboats, Elsah became a backwater.

Now the hamlet is thoroughly spruced up. A pair of narrow, parallel streets run halfway along its length, merging before a one-lane stone bridge. The white frame United Methodist Church would feel comfortable in New England. Tiny flower-filled yards surround restored stone houses. The smell of fresh bread and pastries floats from the award-winning Elsah Landing Restaurant, whose changing menu features homemade soups and an array of pies and cheesecakes. If it's not time for a meal, you can pick up breads, rolls, jams, and jellies at its bakery next door.

Several Elsah homes have become bed and breakfasts, including the Green Tree Inn run by Mary Ann and Michael Pitchford. All nine rooms are decorated in nineteenth-century style and have balconies. An 1850s-style shop downstairs displays herbs, teas, pottery, linens, and laces on old store counters and cupboards. Mary Ann clues guests in on what's in season at nearby fruit- and berry-picking farms, the whereabouts of a shiitake mushroom grower, how to find stables, or how to charter a 1938 motor-yacht for an afternoon on the river. She's also happy to give advice to visitors who are just passing through.

Two miles past Elsah, the old-time, members-only resort of Chautauqua is tucked at the base of the bluffs, buffered from the highway by a miniature lighthouse and rowboat-sized marina. The Victorian dignity of Chautauqua's spacious summer homes magnifies the tackiness of Raging Rivers water park another mile along, where 1,000 feet of baby-blue water slides mar the bluffs.

In another mile, the half-restored village of Grafton straggles along the Mississippi just below its junction with the Illinois River. You can buy live bait and fried fish wrapped in newspaper and launch your boat at a landing also frequented by ducks, coots, and kingfishers. The *Gazetteer of Illinois* of 1834 summed up Grafton as a "post office, one store, one tavern, and a number of families." In those days, the ambitious village hoped to become a great river port. Nowadays it looks to tourists to give the economy a boost.

Down at Grafton's old boat works on Front Street, Mariner Junction rents bicycles, fishing boats, and jet skis. The *Belle of Grafton* excursion boat docks next door. Along Main Street (Route 100), many of the stone and brick houses and businesses have been tidied up as antique shops, restaurants, inns, and other establishments. A Greek Revival general store from the 1840s is now Golden Eagle Antiques; city hall also occupies a former store.

The Grafton Lumber Co. Mall houses several shops selling antiques and collectibles, plus the woodworking studio of Richard Mosby, who owns the building. Mosby's specialty is nineteenth-century furniture— cribs, wardrobes, tables, cupboards. "People from Grafton go elsewhere for such pieces,"

Mosby told me. "People from elsewhere come to me." If it's time to eat when you visit Grafton, try out Brainerd's Village Inn, noted for its pies and cobblers, or the Fin Inn, which has 8,000 gallons worth of aquariums that Mississippi River fish and turtles call home. (Or continue five miles on Route 100 to the lodge at Pere Marquette State Park, which we'll visit later in this route; its Sunday brunch is a particularly good value.)

If you're up for some fresh produce or other farm products, take a side trip along Route 3, which threads inland from Grafton along a winding, wooded hollow that opens into the gentle hills of farm-market and U-pick country. Though apples are the favored crop, you'll also find peaches, plums, pumpkins, pears, and all kinds of berries, as well as jams, jellies, apple butter, and cider for sale. The Greater Alton Convention and Visitors Bureau has a brochure with a map listing many of the major orchards and markets in this area and in Calhoun County.

Leave Grafton on Route 100. The road now cuts through a narrow floodplain between the Illinois River and its bluffs. In just a mile or two you reach the Brussels Ferry. It's free and operates twenty-four hours a day. The flat boats land at the pointed tip of skinny Calhoun County alongside a row of houses on stilts. Go straight ahead. At first you'll pass through the flat bottomlands at the junction of the Illinois and Mississippi rivers where sloughs and lakes have been set aside as fishing and hunting reserves. Soon the road rises into the rolling hills that shelter family farms and orchards and then into Brussels.

When you're almost to Brussels, turn left at the Golden Eagle post office (an orchard will be on your right, and a sign points you toward the *Golden Eagle Ferry*). The road meanders over hills squeezed between the two rivers. When the orchards are in bloom—and in fall when the trees turn to blazing colors—the landscape looks like a crumpled quilt.

Turn up the short, steep driveway of Cresswell Cemetery to stand among 150 years of tombstones and drink in the sweeping vistas to the south and east.

The road continues over the rolling terrain, then swoops downhill to end at the *Golden Eagle Ferry*. This genuine paddle wheeler hauls cars and passengers back and forth across the Mississippi to St. Charles County, Missouri, at $4.00 per car. You can take this short nostalgia trip or watch the riverboat from Kinder's Restaurant next to the dock. Back uphill, you'll

The Brussels Ferry crossing the Illinois River

find fruit and vegetable stands and farms selling jelly, apple butter, and eggs.

In Brussels, the rambling Wittmond Hotel is locally famous more for its low-cost, family-style food than for its aging rooms. Built in 1847 as a trading post, it later became a stagecoach stop. I entered the Wittmond through its long, narrow bar, squeezing by four hefty beer-drinking good old boys in bib overalls. The room next door is a dusty flea market of clothes, horse collars, and other used items plus a few household supplies like Pine Sol, fly spray, mustard, and Mai Tai mix. The restaurant, in the back, is decorated with a cross and pictures of presidents Richard Nixon and John F. Kennedy. None of the dishes match, and on weekends they're washed up by three or four women rather than an automatic dishwasher. However, people line up for a chance to enjoy the bountiful home-cooked meals the Wittmond puts out.

Brussels also supports a craft shop, a tea room serving German meals and pastries, another Kinder's Restaurant, a Red & White Food Store, a tavern or two, and an American Legion hall.

Go straight ahead through Brussels, on past the red brick St. Mary's church. At the edge of town the road curves left, then right again just before St. Matthew's Lutheran Church, where tombstones come almost up to the front door of the neighboring parsonage. The road rolls over the hills and descends to the Illinois River bottomlands, heading toward Hardin and Kampsville. Farms crouch at the base of hills and bluffs to the west. Some are neat as a pin; more, regrettably, are down-at-the-heels or abandoned.*

As you approach the county seat of Hardin, quarries have chomped big bites out of the limestone bluffs. Hardin's water tower and cemetery overlook the town, where bait and

*For an alternate route to Kampsville along the Mississippi River side of Calhoun County, see page 121.

tackle shops are more common than taverns or gas stations. Birdhouses and picnic tables sit beside the riverbank south of an old lift bridge. Hardin has only 1,100 residents, but it's the center of this apple-growing region (just across the bridge is Ringhausen's Apple Shed). County offices still fit in the modest red brick building erected in 1848.

Continue north. You're now on Route 100, which followed the eastern shore of the Illinois River and crossed it at Hardin. At the north edge of town, the locally popular Barefoot Bar sits on the riverbank across the road from Calhoun High School. You'll sight more U-pick spots, well-kept homes, and farms both tidy and tumbledown on the way into Kampsville.

Alternate Route to Kampsville

The Mississippi River side of Calhoun County seems as remote as anywhere in the state. To get there, turn west (left) at a sign for the Winfield Ferry, roughly seven miles north of Brussels. In Batchtown, turn right at the second stop sign. The narrow blacktop affords occasional river views as it leads north across hills and squeezes over low bridges. Several centennial farms, (in the same family for a hundred years or more) lie along the route. These and most of the other homesteads raise hogs, though you'll also spot a few cattle and sheep.

At Gilead, a sign in front of a trailer announces that this was the first county seat from the 1820s, until it was moved to Hardin in 1848. In its early days, Calhoun County was heavily wooded, and its lumberjack population was so unruly that a bill to abolish the county almost passed the state assembly of 1836–1837. During those early days, John Shaw, known as the "Black Prince," ran a country store, speculated in land, and rigged county elections in which he was named commissioner. He was later deposed and fled the region.

More hills and river views precede your arrival in Hamburg, a rumpled town with a tiny park, a café, and a few former shops converted to homes. Continue north along the Mississippi to Route 96, where you turn east (right) to Kampsville.

Kampsville has several antiques and craft shops, plus a small but well organized archaeological museum that tells the story of prehistoric Indian life uncovered during three decades of nearby digging. Turn east (right) on Route 96 toward the Kampsville Inn Restaurant next to a free ferry back across the Illinois River.

Follow Route 108 to the little town of Eldred, hunched under wooded limestone outcrops. Turn north (left) on Eldred Road (locally called Bluff Road), the first paved road you come to; the bluffs will be on your right. Four miles north, Bill and Lindy Hobson operate Bluffdale Vacation Farm. A working farm that has been in Bill's family for more than 165 years, its centerpiece is a stone house built in 1828 by his great-great grandfather, who reportedly welcomed the touring British author Charles Dickens as a guest. "The dining room fireplace is big enough to roast a whole deer," Lindy stated. Guests stay in air-conditioned rooms or suites and enjoy a heated pool, hot tub, playground, horseback riding, hiking, and boat rides, plus helping out with farm chores like feeding the chickens and pigs or gathering eggs.

Eldred Road travels south from Eldred along limestone cliffs cut by stream-eroded valleys, passing hog farms, an old grain elevator, a country cemetery, and more orchards. Continue south (left) when you reach Route 100, traveling through Nutwood before reaching the river's edge at Pere Marquette State Park.

The Civilian Conservation Corps built the park's lodge during the Depression and the 700-ton fireplace in the soaring fifty-foot-high lobby remains its showstopper. Twenty-two of the original stone guest houses are behind the lodge, with additional rooms and a swimming pool added during a recent renovation. The park also has a marina, riding stables, camping facilities, and hiking trails.

Behind the lodge, roads lead uphill and across wooded ridges mantled with loess, the dust laid down during the last Ice Age. From viewpoints atop the bluffs, you can take a last look across the soft hills of Calhoun County before heading back toward Alton and St. Louis.

In the Area

Southern Illinois Tourism Council, P.O. Box 40, Whittington, IL 62897: 618-629-2506 or 800-342-3100

Greater Alton/Twin Rivers Convention and Visitors Bureau, 200 Piasa Street, Alton, IL 62002: 800-258-6445

Elsah Landing Restaurant (Elsah): 618-374-1607

Green Tree Inn (Elsah): 618-374-2821 (reservations)
Mary Ann and Michael Pitchford: 618-374-2520 (general inquiries)

Belle of Grafton (excursion boat, Grafton): 618-786-2318

Brainerd's Village Inn (Grafton): 618-786-2282

Fin Inn (Grafton): 618-786-2030

Bluffdale Vacation Farm (Eldred): 217-983-2854

Pere Marquette State Park: 618-786-3323

Pere Marquette Lodge: 618-786-2331

11 ~

Cahokia to Chester:

Three Heritages

From St. Louis: Take I-55/I-70 east to exit 6, turn south on Route 111, then east on Collinsville Road to the site of Cahokia Mounds State Historic Site.

From Springfield: Take I-55 south to exit 6 as above. This trip begins just across the Mississippi River from St. Louis.

Highlights: *Pre-Columbian Indian history at Cahokia Mounds; French exploration and settlement history at Fort de Chartres State Historic Site and elsewhere; German settlements and historic places; a smorgasbord of things to do and see: the Liberty Bell of the West, a Popeye statue and annual Popeye Picnic, a horseradish festival, antiques and country stores, a covered bridge, and outdoor recreational activities.*

The longest distances on this southwestern Illinois route are those spanning time. We begin eleven centuries ago at the site of the largest pre-Columbian Indian city north of Mexico on the fertile Mississippi River plain across from St. Louis, Missouri. We next skip 800 years to the first settlements founded in Illinois along the river by French explorers, missionaries, and soldiers. Then we jump to the nineteenth century, when the region's rich land drew farmers and craftsmen from Germany. Our route visits the only Illinois territory *west* of the Mississippi and concludes in the hometown of the spinach-eating cartoon sailor, Popeye.

124

Sometime after A.D. 850, Mississippian Indians began work on what would become North America's most massive prehistoric earthen construction. It took 300 years for laborers to haul 22 million cubic feet of earth—basket by basket—to create a four-tiered platform rising 100 feet from its fourteen-acre base. On top sat a government and ceremonial center overlooking a sun calendar made of upright logs—a Stonehenge of wood—that measured seasons and scheduled rituals.

This great mound was the center of a prehistoric city whose remains lie at Cahokia Mounds State Historic and World Heritage Site, the start of our route.

Reaching a population of 20,000 and covering six square miles, Cahokia was the largest prehistoric city north of Mexico, complete with surrounding suburbs. But by 1500 it was abandoned; nobody knows why, or what became of its people.

The story of Cahokia Mounds and the sun-worshipping people who built a metropolis there comes to life in vivid detail at the site's 33,000-square-foot interpretive center. Multimedia exhibits, including an engrossing fifteen-projector slide show and a scale model of the city, examine the everyday activities of Cahokia's residents. You can also walk through a life-size diorama to see men butchering a deer carcass, youngsters playing, and women grinding corn. You'll smell the prairie grass used to construct homes. Outside, you can hike to the top of imposing Monk's Mound and stroll among some of the sixty-five other mounds remaining on the site.

The name of the original city is unknown. It was called Cahokia after a tribe belonging to the Illini Confederation of Indians who lived in the area when the first French missionaries arrived. Father Jean Francois Buisson de St. Cosme, a French Canadian, gave the same name to the riverside trading village he founded in 1698 ten miles southeast of the mounds. To get there, head west on Collinsville Road to I-255, then south to Route 157 (Camp Jackson Road); go west again to Route 3. At this intersection stands what remains of the French outpost. Of the half dozen French settlements along this stretch of the Mississippi, Cahokia became the center of Indian trade.

In 1699, Father St. Cosme constructed the Church of the Holy Family, the first one west of the Alleghenies. Although it burned down, salvaged beams were used in an altar section of the replacement erected in 1799. This small, well-proportioned house of worship was built in the Canadian post-on-foundation palisade style, in which the hand-hewn walnut logs are placed upright.

Just southwest of the intersection stands a four-room residence believed to have been constructed in 1737 by Captain Jean Baptiste Saucier, builder of Fort de Chartres (further south on our route). In 1793, St. Clair County purchased the building, made of upright logs with a cantilevered roof extending over four porches, "to act as a jail, pillory, whipping post and stocks" and to serve as the center of government for an area extending north to Canada. The first U.S. court sessions and the first elections in Illinois were held in the Cahokia courthouse.

Head south from Cahokia on Route 3, which merges into I-255. When I-255 turns west to cross the Mississippi, stay on Route 3, following signs toward downtown Columbia, a town that reflects the German heritage predominant among nineteenth-century settlers in Monroe County.* Columbia sits safely at the edge of bluffs overlooking the Mississippi floodplain. Its sturdy, *Hausfrau*-neat brick houses lead off Main Street where the Columbia Haus serves schnitzels amid a collection of Bavarian beer steins. A sign extends the traditional Bavarian and Austrian greeting, "Gruss Gott."

* For an alternate route through pure country to Maeystown, see page 129.

Continue on Route 3 to Waterloo. Home of a winery by the same name, Waterloo preserves the Peterstown House stagecoach stop built in the 1830s on the sixty-mile Kaskaskia-Cahokia Trail. The white frame Connecticut-style building is now a museum and country store with two pioneer log cabins out back. Belle Fontaine, at the end of Church Street, is the spot where Revolutionary War veterans of George Rogers Clark's command organized the first permanent American settlement in the Northwest Territories in 1782. By 1800, Belle Fontaine's population of 286 made it the third largest community in the Illinois Territory.

On Saturday mornings, you can browse a farmers market on Waterloo's shady courthouse square or devour some goodies from Ahne's Bakery at Mill and Church streets. Leave town going west on Route 156 (Fourth Street), past German-style brick businesses and homes. Just past a park at the edge of town, turn south (left) at signs toward Wartburg and Maeystown.

The roads along here aren't laid out in the neat checkerboard squares platted on the flat prairies. Instead, they curve and wander through undulating terrain divided into farm fields and wooded plots. Wartburg, population 54, was named for the castle where Martin Luther translated the Bible into German. The 1863 Holy Cross Lutheran Church shows the work of outstanding masons, while the seventy-five-foot-tall steeple, added in 1874, seems less skillfully constructed.

Turn off the Maeystown Road onto Ahne Road at the White House Café in Wartburg. In a mile or two, you'll sight the ruined Old Baum Church to your right. The melancholy stone church, now roofless, lasted from 1883 until its abandonment in 1938. Overgrown mid-nineteenth century graves of the Sparwasser family lie across the road.

Follow Ahne Road to a stone farm near the intersection with County Road KK. Just to the right is Madonnaville, where the graves around Immaculate Conception Church outnumber the residents. Like Wartburg, it was a village founded on religion. The 1856 Roman Catholic church and several nearby buildings are more examples of work by the superb German masons who settled the area.

From the Madonnaville church, go back to Ahne Road, but continue straight ahead, traveling east on County KK, which leads back to Maeystown Road. Turn south (right) and curve into Maeystown, a village terraced into the hillsides above a creek by German immigrants. Placed on the National Register of Historic Districts in 1978, Maeystown boasts an ensemble of buildings dating from the mid-1800s to early 1900s. The log homestead and later home of village founder Jacob Maeys lie along the creek just before a narrow stone bridge leading into town. Here you'll see original details such as flagstone gutters and smokehouses, as well as the town's first log church (1859) next to the steepled stone house of worship built six years later. A general store and cobbler's from 1899 is now a gift and collectibles shop; an 1857 brick-maker's home and tavern now sells antiques.

Weekenders are drawn by the Corner George Inn, a bed and breakfast owned by David and Marcia Braswell. They restored an 1883 hotel and saloon opened by George Jacob Hoffmann and completed by his wife Sibilla after his death. But the inn took its name from another George Hoffmann— no relation to George Jacob—known as "Corner George." He lived in the building and ran a general store in the former saloon from 1907 to 1914, and his nickname distinguished him from three other George Hoffmanns living in Maeystown at the time.

The inn's five rooms are outfitted in antiques mixed with family heirlooms, enhanced by Victorian wallpaper, quilts, and bathrooms with clawfoot tubs. The Braswells' favorite room is the summer kitchen, redone as a guest cottage. There are two sitting rooms, plus a bright, spacious upstairs ballroom with ornate embroidered rugs, a fainting couch, and an 1880s dining room table that belonged to David's great-great-grandfather. Downstairs, the general store is in business again, this time offering handicrafts and gifts.

Kitty-corner from the Corner George, Hoefft's Village Inn has a daily sandwich special that's usually $3.00 or less. The main dining room is in the rear. If you choose to sit in the dark wood bar up front, you may share space with local good old boys playing poker or rolling dice with their rounds of beer.

Those willing to exchange some old towns, antique shops, and historic sites for country roads might try the Bluff Road route to Maeystown. Shortly after exiting I-255 onto Route 3 toward Columbia is a right turn onto Bluff Road. The blacktop leads along the wooded limestone bluffs, sometimes cutting across the wide floodplain. The view west extends for miles across the flat farm fields to forested hills marking the opposite side of the Mississippi valley. The landscape is particularly beautiful during the fall foliage season. Our main route passes through somewhat similar terrain south of Maeystown; this alternate route is for travelers who can't get enough pure country.

Leave Maeystown on Mill Street. In about two miles, be on the lookout for an easy-to-miss turn south (left) onto Bluff Road; it's immediately before the small, unmarked hamlet of Chalfin Bridge. You'll know you're headed the right way if the bluffs are on your left. Farms nestle against the steep limestone banks, their fields spread toward the river. In warm weather, turkey vultures might be circling high above.

Train tracks parallel the blacktop road and the village of Fults parallels the railroad line. At Prairie du Rocher, turn toward the river at signs pointing to Fort de Chartres State Historic Site, about four miles away.

The stone fort was erected in 1753 to replace a palisade of squared logs built in 1720. It served as France's governmental headquarters for the vast Illinois Country extending from lakes Michigan and Superior to the Ohio and Missouri rivers. This was the last place the French flag flew in the New World: it was lowered in 1765, two years after the official end of the French and Indian War when British troops finally took possession.

The partially rebuilt fort comes complete with bastions, a gatehouse, and a powder magazine considered by many to be the oldest building in Illinois. Barracks, guardhouses, a government house, and a storehouse (which serves as a museum) complete the fort. Every June, some 1,500 area residents play the roles of French fur trappers and buckskinners, traders, friendly Indians, and military, setting up tents and tepees for a two-day Rendezvous that draws 35,000 visitors. It's abuzz with shooting competitions, military drills, dancing, music, food, and traders. Other equally exciting events, including a Revolutionary War encampment, Kids' Day, French and Indian War assemblage, and winter rendezvous, are held almost monthly throughout the year. In addition, tours are provided by guides in period French Marine attire.

Return to Prairie du Rocher, a somnolent hamlet founded about 1722. It claims the title of oldest town in Illinois, since other settlements began as missions, forts, or trading posts and *evolved* into villages. French was spoken by most residents as late as 1900. The sturdy brick St. Joseph's Church started out as a mission in 1731; its cemetery has burials of Indians, slaves, French and American settlers, and recent residents.

At the other end of town, the modern village hall was built in the French palisade style with a high roof and uncomfortable seats for the town council. Creole House, a long white frame building begun in 1800, is a French colonial residence with a wide front porch. If you're hungry, Aubuchon's grocery store across the street makes pile-it-on sandwiches. For more inventive cooking (or a place to stay), La Maison du Rocher receives kudos throughout the region. The oldest part of the building was constructed of limestone blocks taken from the walls of Fort de Chartres.

Continue southeast on Bluff Road. Within a few miles, you'll notice overhangs at the base of the bluffs where farmers shelter hay, equipment, calves, lambs, and wood. Hunter-gatherer Indians also used these overhangs as shelters—more than 8,000 years ago. A plaque alongside the road just before Modoc marks such a spot. At Modoc, a right turn for Kellogg takes you to a $4.00 ferry ride ($1.00 if you don't take your car) across the Mississippi to historic St. Genevieve, Missouri, where many French in the region resettled after the French and Indian War.

Just after Roots, you'll cross the Kaskaskia River upstream from its confluence with the Mississippi. The river is known locally as "Peabody's Ditch," since it was channelized to barge coal from the Peabody Coal Company mines upriver.

The road heads east to Ellis Grove and the intersection with Route 3, marked by Scheffer's Meat Market, an old-time establishment selling German-style sausages and cheese. There you turn south (right). When you reach Fort Kaskaskia Road, turn west (right) to Fort Kaskaskia State Historic Site and the Pierre Menard home, which look out over the watery grave of old Kaskaskia village.

Go first to the home of Pierre Menard below the bluffs. Menard was a French Canadian trader who in the early 1790s arrived in Kaskaskia, a town that got its start in 1703 as a French settlement and trading post.

In 1800, Menard began construction of his home, a beautifully proportioned frame structure with wide porches set against the hillside. A detached kitchen, a smokehouse, a springhouse, a privy, and a garden are out back. When you go inside, it's clear that Menard was very well-to-do. The home is adorned with an elegant Aubusson carpet, original mantelpieces, a portrait of the entrepeneur at age seventy-two, his secretary-bookcase, and other period furnishings.

In 1809, Kaskaskia became the capital of the Illinois Territory and went on to become the first state capital in 1818, when Pierre Menard was elected lieutenant governor.

From the state park above the home, maps help you envision how the Mississippi River went on a rampage in 1881, eventually appropriating the Kaskaskia River's channel and wiping out most of the old capital in the process. Almost 4,000 caskets from Kaskaskia's three cemeteries were moved to the safety of Garrison Hill in the park, their headstones placed on the slope toward the river.

Return to Route 3 and turn south (right) toward Chester. If you want to stock up on strawberries, peaches, apples, or other seasonal fruits and vegetables, stop at Colvis Orchards. In October, Colvis decorates for Halloween and sets up kids' games (such as a maze made of straw bales); before Christmas, you can cut your own tree.

When you reach Chester's outskirts, you might choose to take the seventeen-mile journey to the present-day village of Kaskaskia on the only piece of Illinois territory lying *west* of the Mississippi. Turn west (right) on Route 150 and cross the bridge into Missouri, where the road becomes Route 51. Go to County Road H and turn north (right) to St. Marys, where you turn right again at signs for Kaskaskia Bell. Cross a one-lane bridge and you're in Illinois again. The village lies on levee-protected bottomlands.

In Kaskaskia, you'll find the bronze "Liberty Bell of the West," cast in France in 1741 as a gift from the king. The bell was rung on July 4, 1778, to proclaim the capture of old Kaskaskia from the British by George Rogers Clark's militia without a shot being fired. Down the street, the peeling false front of Old Kaskaskia Trading Post advertises "souvenirs, postcards, tourist info., flea mkt., art & crafts, snacks." Every year the town puts on an old-fashioned Fourth-of-July celebration with band concerts, patriotic speeches, and picnics spread across the lawn.

Retrace your route to the Illinois end of the Mississippi bridge, where Popeye creator and Chester native Elzie Crisler Segar is saluted with a statue of the cartoon sailor. As you wind through town, you can stop at the modern blufftop

Kaskaskia, Illinois—west *of the Mississippi*

Randolph County Courthouse to ascend its double-helix stairwell to an observatory. The squat, solid former courthouse next door was built in the Civil War era to withstand Confederate cannonballs. Now it's a county museum containing everything from eighteenth-century French documents to an electric chair once used in Menard State Prison—with a list of those who died in it.

After viewing that grisly exhibit, you may need to regain your strength. So our route ends at the Robin's Nest gift shop on Swanwick Street. This is headquarters for the Popeye Fan Club, where you can purchase a 79¢ can of spinach emblazoned with his portrait. That ought to pep you right up.

Other Sights to See

Those wanting to spend more time in this region will find many additional places and events to enjoy. Here's a sampler:

Collinsville

- April's Horseradish Festival celebrates the crop that's made Collinsville the Horseradish Capital of the World: ninety percent of the world's horseradish is grown in this area.

Belleville

- National Shrine of Our Lady of the Snows, 9500 W. Illinois Highway 15, is one of the largest outdoor shrines in the United States operated by the Missionary Oblates of Mary Immaculate.
- Visit Eckert's Country Store & Farms, 3101 Greenmount Road, for U-pick apples, a fresh fruit and vegetable market, a frozen custard stand, a butcher shop, a bakery, wagon rides, a petting farm, and special events.

Red Bud

- This rural German town has a number of antique shops plus excellent examples of nineteenth-century architecture, including its city hall. The *North County News,* in a storefront near the intersection of Routes 3 and 154, displays some antique toys in its lobby.

Kaskaskia River State Fish and Wildlife Area

- North of Route 154 east of Red Bud, this preserve encompasses Baldwin Lake, a cooling lake for a power plant. "Catfish get as big as hogs in there!" say local fishermen.

Ruma

- St. Patrick's Catholic Church, built in 1864, has a schoolhouse and a moody cemetery. The Adorers of the Blood of Christ Convent, next door to St. Patrick's, is a retirement home for nuns who produce superb quilts, handicrafts, jams, jellies, and other items for sale at a September bazaar. You'll also find a small craft shop at the convent, but it's advisable to call ahead to be sure it's open, particularly if you're with a large group.

Evansville

- An old Kaskaskia River town along Route 3, Evansville boasts a large public dock and boat access area, camping facilities, excellent waterskiing, and The Family Tradition restaurant specializing in seafood.

- The one-room Charter Oak School, east of Evansville on County Highway 4, was built in 1873 with octagonal sides to let more daylight in and to offer greater stability in case of high winds or tornados. It sits alone in a field next to former strip mines, and is the scene of an August cornfest.

Sparta

- Sparta lies east of Ruma and Evansville at routes 4 and 154. Its train station was a backdrop for the 1966 movie *In the Heat of the Night* starring Sidney Poitier and Rod Steiger. The station has just been restored as a museum for the pencil drawings of artist Roscoe Misselhorn. A small historical district comprised of big brick homes offers a Southern touch under old oak trees.

Bremen

- Along Route 150 east of Chester, St. Mary's covered bridge was built in 1854 on the Bremen–Chester plank toll road and used until 1930. Except for the floor, all of its original timber is intact.

Turkey Bluffs and Rockwood

- South of Chester on Route 3, Turkey Bluffs Scenic Overlook is a great spot for picnics, hikes, horseback rides, and views over the Mississippi. Rockwood, four miles further south, was a beginning point for slaves escaping along the Underground Railroad.

In the Area

It is easy to enjoy this route as a day-trip from St. Louis or other Illinois and Missouri cities and towns. However, if you're coming from further afield and will need a place to

stay, the villages and towns on and near our route do not
have a large number of motel and bed and breakfast rooms.
During special events such as the Rendezvous at Fort de
Chartres, the Popeye Picnic in Chester, and drag-boat
racing competitions on the Kaskaskia River at Evansville,
area motels may be full. On those busy weekends, you'll
need to reserve rooms well in advance if you want to stay
in a spot along the route. The tourism offices can advise
you on which dates accommodations may be hard to find
and where rooms are likeliest to be available.

Southwestern Illinois Tourism and Convention Bureau
(Highland): 618-654-3556 or 800-782-9587

Southern Illinois Regional Tourism Council (Whittington):
618-629-2506 or 800-342-3100

Collinsville Convention and Visitors Bureau: 618-345-4999

Cahokia Mounds State Historic and World Heritage Site
(Collinsville): 618-346-5160

Cahokia Courthouse and Church of the Holy Family:
618-332-1782

Peterstown House (Waterloo): 618-939-8227

Corner George Inn Bed and Breakfast (Maeystown):
618-458-6660

La Maison du Rocher Restaurant and Bed and Breakfast
(Prairie du Rocher): 618-284-3463

Fort de Chartres State Historic Site: 618-284-7230

Fort Kaskaskia State Historic Site (Ellis Grove): 618-859-3741

Pierre Menard Home (Ellis Grove): 618-859-3031

Randolph County Museum (Chester): 618-826-2510

National Shrine of Our Lady of the Snows (Belleville):
618-397-6700

Eckert's Country Store and Farms crop hotline (Belleville):
618-234-4406

The Adorers of the Blood of Christ Convent (Ruma):
618-282-3848

12 ~

The Great Southwest

From Chicago: Take I-57 south for about 315 miles; then take Route 13 west to Carbondale.

From St. Louis: Take I-64 east to Route 51 south to Carbondale.

Highlights: *Civil War history; Shawnee National Forest, Oakwood Bottoms/Green Tree Reservoir, La Rue-Pine Hills Ecological Area, Cache River territory, Trail of Tears State Forest, and Giant City State Park; the "Goose Capital of the World" and the World War II hero pig, King Neptune; vineyards, vegetables, and a peach festival.*

Illinois is wedged firmly into the South. Cairo, at the tip of the state, lies forty-one miles farther south than Richmond, capital of the Confederacy. Many Illinois pioneers were southerners from Kentucky, Tennessee, and the Carolinas. Southern tupelos and cypress trees rise from the turbid swamps that formed in the floodplains of the Ohio and Mississippi rivers. Above the swamps, the uplifts and folds of 300-million-year-old sandstone formed the Illinois Ozarks. This east–west swath of rugged escarpments, deep canyons, magnificent vistas, and dense woodlands is known as the Shawnee Hills.

Despite its beauty and early settlement, southern Illinois has a history of unfulfilled promise; it was left behind in economic as well as population growth. Its soil was nutrient-poor compared to the rich prairies of central and northern Illinois. Railroads triumphed over rivers as the prime form of transportation by the mid-1800s, making Chicago the major hub and industrial city. Southern Illinois coal mines turned from boom to bust in this century.

Southern Illinois remains overlooked by most visitors, yet those in the know will find a wealth of scenic, recreational, and historical attractions. Spring and fall are the loveliest times to visit any part of southern Illinois. If you plan to spend more than a day on this or the next route ("The Southeast: Hills and History"), it may be best to reserve accommodations ahead.

Carbondale is the closest thing to a big city south of Springfield. As the home of Southern Illinois University, the city's population nearly doubles during the academic year. The campus is functional rather than beautiful, though one end sprawls among ponds and woods. Most commercial business has moved from downtown to malls and shopping strips. Just east of the city's center lies Woodlawn Cemetery, where Civil War General John A. Logan held America's first Memorial Day service in 1855.

No area of Illinois was more torn by the Civil War than its southern tip, which was home to a large number of Confederate sympathizers. Logan, born in neighboring Murphysboro, was pro-South but believed that "the Union must prevail." He fought as a civilian volunteer at Bull Run, then returned home to help end talk of creating a separate, pro-Confederate state out of southern Illinois. Later he joined the Union Army and became the premier volunteer general of the war.

Travel west from Carbondale a few miles on Route 13 to Murphysboro where the John A. Logan Museum, at Edith

Street between 16th and 17th streets, occupies the site of the original Logan Homestead. A faded apple decorates the town's water tower, testifying to the area's juicy fall harvest. An Apple Festival each September features rollicking apple-peeling and apple pie-baking contests along with parades, cider, and an apple queen (with rosy cheeks, one hopes).

Continue west from Murphysboro on Route 149, turn south (left) onto Route 3 at Grimsby, and you've entered the northwest corner of Shawnee National Forest, which covers 260,000 acres of southern Illinois. Although it's one of the nation's smallest national forests, Shawnee contains the most biologically diverse area in the state in a host of preserves, parks, and recreation areas. The natural history here is like pre-Civil War politics: the north and the south overlap.

Route 3 leads south along the flat Mississippi floodplain, which bumps up against the Shawnee Hills to the east. About five miles south of Grimsby, turn east (left) to Oakwood Bottoms/Green Tree Reservoir interpretive center. This area was once cleared and farmed, but the soil was too acidic and heavy to raise crops; now it's returning to its former wetlands state. As I strolled a boardwalk trail over the mushy forest floor, a bluebird almost flew in my face. Other times of the year, the hazard might be one of the 80,000 ducks passing through. This trail and another around a pond are suitable for beginning hikers and disabled people.

Three miles south, a county road leads west to Grand Tower. The Mississippi gouged through the Ozarks here, creating a stretch of river known as "the graveyard" because of all the boats snagged and sunk on the submerged boulders. In 1673, French explorers Louis Jolliet and Father Jacques Marquette planted a cross atop Tower Rock, rising sixty feet on the Missouri side. When the river was dredged to remove

hazards in the late 1800s, this rock was spared because offi-
cials thought it might make a natural foundation for a bridge.
On the Illinois side, rock formations like Devil's Backbone and
Devil's Bake Oven stand like sentinels.

In Grand Tower, Ma Hale's Boarding House Restaurant
has been dishing up family-style meals for half a century on
school lunchroom tables covered in oilcloth. When I stopped
here in 1992, a Sunday dinner of fried chicken, mashed pota-
toes, dumplings, corn, green beans, navy beans, coleslaw,
applesauce, rolls, iced tea, and apple pie (which I declined)
cost $13.28 for two, including tax. Under a tree outside, a
plaque identifies a washbasin carved from a sandstone block
as belonging to Beningsen Boone, a relative of Daniel Boone
and the first white child born in Shawnee County.

Continue south on Route 3. Immediately over the Big
Muddy River, turn east (left) on an unmarked gravel road that
will take you to the 2,525-acre La Rue-Pine Hills Ecological
Area. The road leads to stunning limestone bluffs towering
400 feet over La Rue Swamp. This may be the most biologically diverse nook or cranny in Illinois. Ninety percent of the
mammals found in the state live here, including the rare eastern wood rat—a genuine pack rat. Twenty-three species of
snakes call this home, among them the scarlet snake, copper-
head, mud snake, and water moccasin. Thirty-five percent of
the state's plant species grow here, too, including 1,150 kinds
of ferns, conifers, and flowering plants.

A road leads uphill to scenic overviews of the swamp and
the Mississippi valley and to well-tended nature trails. When
you return to the base of the cliffs, turn south (left) on the
gravel road along the base of the bluffs for a closeup of the
swamp and rock formations. Watch the tree trunks, too. Even
if you don't know one species from another, you'll see great
differences in the shape and texture of bark. In October and

April, this road is closed to allow reptiles safe passage to and from their winter havens in the bluffs where they hibernate. After a mile or so, you can turn west (right) on another gravel road to rejoin Route 3.

In Wolf Lake, watch for a bulldozer graveyard crammed with spare parts and rusting bodies. Five miles later, near the north end of Union County Conservation Area at Ware, signs beckon hunters to clubs and farms where geese are the main targets. A flea market (with emphasis on "flea") marks the

Great Blue Heron
at La Rue Swamp

intersection with Route 146, which leads west across the Mississippi to Cape Girardeau, Missouri. Witz's Village Bar-B-Q, just before the bridge, is known for its lengthy dessert menu and huge Sunday dinner.

On Route 3, you know you've reached Little Egypt, as the state's southern extremity is known, when you enter Thebes. The name was bestowed by Bible-reading farmers from the plains to the north: after losing their corn crop during the wretched weather of 1830–1831, they had to travel to the milder south to purchase seed for the new season—like the sons of Jacob who had "gone down to Egypt for corn."

Alexander County seat from 1835 until 1864 when it was moved south to Cairo, Thebes wore out after its days as a busy river port in the 1880s. The 1846 courthouse, a stark Greek Revival building with slender columns and a two-story portico, perches by itself at the edge of a high bluff overlooking the river and a regrettably run-down part of the town.

South of Thebes, the landscape flattens as you close in on the junction of the Mississippi and Ohio rivers at Cairo. Horseshoe Lake, a Mississippi backwater southwest of Olive Branch, bills itself the "Goose Capital of the World." An estimated 150,000 Canada geese winter at this 2,400-acre, six-foot-deep lake frequented by hunters and fishermen. Photographers and birders also find it fascinating because of the deer, wintering bald eagles, and other forest animals that live against a verdant backdrop of cypress, gum, and swamp cottonwoods. Westside Drive offers some excellent views of the lakes and swamps. If you keep left, you'll reach Eastside Drive, which leads back to Route 3.

The highway joins Route 51 at Future City, named when prospects for this corner of Illinois were light years brighter. Cairo, squeezed onto a narrow peninsula between levees that defend it from the two mighty rivers, was once a major transportation hub. Now most of the barges, visible from Fort Defiance State Park at the Mississippi–Ohio confluence, plow on by as do the freight trains. Cairo is, on the whole, an urban disaster whose population has shrunk from almost 13,500 in the 1930s to 6,300 today. In 1842, English author Charles Dickens described it as "a hotbed of disease, an ugly sepulchre, a grave uncheered by any gleam of promise; a place without one single quality, in earth or air or water, to commend it; such is this dismal Cairo."

But Cairo also had its glory days. In 1867, more than 3,700 steamboats docked at the city. In *Life on the Mississippi* (1883), Mark Twain commented that "Cairo is a brisk town now and is substantially built and has a city look about it." Those days are echoed in a pair of imposing buildings on Washington Avenue (Route 51): the 1884 Safford Memorial Library and Museum and the 1872 Custom House built at a then-stupendous cost of $225,000.

The antique furnishings, marble mantels, and hand-carved bookcases in the preserved Victorian Magnolia Manor at 2700 Washington Street, north of the city's commercial strip, point to the small upper crust that remains in Cairo along what was once known as "Millionaire's Row." Charles A. Galigher, who made his fortune by selling flour to the Union Army, built the mansion, and it was the scene of the greatest social event in Cairo's history: a gala welcome for former president Ulysses S. Grant. Across the street, the Wyndham, a spacious Italianate mansion with verandas and fireplaces, has become a tasteful bed and breakfast.

Retrace the route north on Route 51. Just after crossing the Cache River, the intersection with Route 37 is marked by a U.S. National Military Cemetery. It was established during the Civil War because of the hospital in nearby Mound City that served soldiers wounded in the Battle of Shiloh. More than 2,750 unknown Civil War dead are buried here, along with fifty women who nursed at the hospital. One grave is marked simply "Confederate Spy."

The keels of three Eads iron-clad gunboats were laid at Mound City. Now its downtown area seems to be struggling to survive. Continue north on Route 37 through Olmstead and New Grand Chain into the Cache River territory.

The Cache River starts in the Shawnee Hills near Anna and winds along the valley it carved, supporting wetlands along the way. Then it enters the broad Ohio River valley where it moves sluggishly through what were once even wider wetlands. It supports southern swamps as well as northern plants that are relicts of the Ice Age. But humans hated those soggy spots and decided to drain them, and loggers chopped away at the old-growth forests along the river's path.

Then conservationists—inside and outside the state bureaucracy—got to work to preserve some of the sloughs, swamps, and forests, gradually adding acreage to form protected natural areas. Now reforestation and restoration of the river are under way.

Among the areas where you can hike is Limekiln Springs on the lower Cache River where clear springs feed a slough favored by waterfowl. Developed by The Nature Conservancy, a one-mile trail leads through oak, hickory, sugar maple, black walnut, and other trees (some gnawed by beavers), where you might spot the elusive pileated woodpecker, great horned owls, wood ducks, and tree frogs. There are boardwalks in spots, but parts of the trail may be muddy. To get there, turn west (left) off Route 37 at signs directing you to Shawnee College. Go approximately four-and-a-half miles to the gravel Cache Chapel Road, where you turn north (right). The road ends in a parking lot where the trail begins.

Continue north on Route 37 from Shawnee College Road to Route 149, where you turn east (right) to Karnak, which was largely a company-built logging town. Woodsmen of the World Lodge 657 and Corzini's Pool Hall offer residents recreation. Go north from Karnak to Belknap, another logging town. Signs point you toward Cache River State Natural Area headquarters, where you can pick up maps, and to Little Black Slough/Heron Pond.

The easygoing mile-and-a-half Heron Pond trail crosses the Cache River on a suspension bridge, and follows its course through hardwood forests to a floating boardwalk into the pond where dense stands of cypress and tupelo grow. The trail then loops through the forest and back alongside the swamp. The park is thick with wildlife—great blue and green herons, thrushes, woodpeckers, warblers, raccoons, minks, foxes, deer, and coyotes. Naturalists have also seen signs of bobcats and river otters.

When you return from the park to the county road, turn east (left) to US 45 then north (left again) to Vienna. This county seat's courthouse square features headstones carved by the J.W. Monument Co., which advertises itself as "The company you've heard about all your life." Aficionados of Illinois political history can visit the home of Vienna's most famous citizen, former Illinois secretary of state Paul Powell, at Route 146 and Vine Street. Powell's classic political utterance was: "I smell the meat a'cookin'." When he died in 1970, $800,000 in cash was found in shoe boxes in his Springfield hotel room.

Travel west from Vienna on Route 146. In six miles, you'll cross the Cache River again, and in another four miles or so, turn north (right) on Mt. Pleasant Road toward some world-class potato chips. They're sold at Good's Old Fashioned Foods, a country business operated by a Mennonite family. The sign over the employee entrance from the shop to the factory exhorts, "Keep thyself pure." The kettle-cooked chips have great texture and crispiness.

Back on Route 146 west, a sign points to a historical marker on the south side of the highway just before I-57. Pull in and pay your respects to hero pig King Neptune. During World War II, a local businessman saw school kids raising "Victory Pigs" to auction for war bonds. So he successfully bid on a 265-pound porker and named him King Neptune. He painted the pig's nails red, outfitted him in a crown and purple robe, and traveled the Midwest auctioning him for war bonds over and over. King Neptune died of old age several years after the Allied victory, and the inscription on his tombstone reads: "Buried here—King Neptune, famous Navy mascot pig auctioned for $19,000,000.00 in war bonds 1942–1946 to help make a free world."

Follow Route 146 into Anna and Jonesboro, snuggled together at the edge of gorgeous Shawnee Hills countryside. The two towns share a population of 8,200 and several motels. Continue west to Route 127 and turn north (right) to Trail of Tears State Forest. As the peaceful forest road passes wooded limestone bluffs, it's difficult to imagine the heartbreaking event that occurred here. Between mid-December 1838 and early March 1839, 10,000 Cherokee Indians were forced to move 800 miles from the Great Smokies to an Oklahoma reservation. Because of floating ice in the Mississippi, they had to stop here in makeshift camps that offered little shelter from an unusually severe winter. Many of them died. Today, the Trail of Tears park has lovely hiking and bridle paths.

Further north on Route 127, turn west (left) and snake uphill to the top of Bald Knob Mountain, where a massive cross of white porcelain-on-steel panels rises 110 feet from the Shawnee Forest's most prominent elevation. Financed by interdenominational donations, the cross commands a 360-degree view over 600 square miles of hills and valleys—the most panoramic in Illinois and at its most magnificent during fall foliage season.

Zigzag downhill, then uphill again into Alto Pass, where you'll find several antique shops. Alto Vineyards, in the hills off Route 127, has won many awards for the wines produced from its French-American hybrid vines. From Alto Pass, a blacktop country road winds to Cobden, with a picnic site and long views over leafy hills along the way.

Cobden calls itself "The Apple Knocker Town," and it has always been a center for fruit and vegetable growing with markets like Draper Produce. Set in a gap in the hills, Cobden is cut down the center by railroad tracks with bridges connecting the two downtown streets that run parallel to the line. A tiny museum lies on one side of the tracks. On the other side you'll find the Crystal Café, where a lunch of home-style ham and beans costs $3.25. On Front Street, Lawrence Box and Basket Factory is one of the largest producers of fruit baskets in the country, using equipment that dates back to the last century. They say it's the only place in the world where round-bottom baskets are still made. Though deviating from its Apple Knocker nickname, Cobden's August Peach Festival is its most famous event; you can pig out on fresh peach cobbler and yummy peach ice cream.

Go east from Cobden to Route 51, then north (left) to Makanda Road, which leads east (right) into Makanda. Makanda's Boardwalk, a clump of circa 1890s storefronts, houses half a dozen businesses. Among them you'll find antiques and reproductions, rental bicycles, ice cream, sandwiches, and some outstanding arts and crafts such as handsome braided rugs and bronze art pieces.

Makanda sits on the edge of 3,700-acre Giant City State Park, centering on an oak-and-limestone lodge constructed by the Civilian Conservation Corps in the 1930s. On an eighty-foot cliff not far from the main entrance are the remains of a Native American stone fort erected between A.D. 600 and 800. The park's most remarkable feature, though, is its "city" of natural sandstone blocks arranged on neatly eroded "streets." There are tiny beauties, too—lush ferns, mosses, and hundreds of kinds of wildflowers draping the stone boulders and walls. Indians used the overhanging rock shelters, worn into the sides of cliffs, as long as 10,000 years ago. During the Civil War, these shelters were havens for Confederate sympathizers.

Leave the park toward Carbondale and Route 13. Go approximately eight miles to Little Grassy Road and turn east (right) at signs toward Little Grassy and Crab Orchard lakes, and several other reservoirs. Half a million Canada geese winter in this wildlife refuge, whose waters are stocked with bass, bluegills, trout, sunfish, catfish, crappies, carp, and yellow perch. The road winds among lakes and reservoirs dotted with marinas, scout and church camps, and nature trails. When you reach a sign pointing right toward Crab Orchard Lake Information Center, follow its directions. You'll reach Route 148, on which you turn north (left), to travel through the heart of the reserve and across Crab Orchard Lake. Turn east again (right) on Old Route 13, toward Marion.

At the intersection of routes 148 and 13, Wye Supply inhabits a sagging building crammed with crafts, hardware, life jackets, frying pans, roach killer, and everything else under the sun. It has the aura of a dusty junk store though most of its merchandise is new. If browsing's not to your taste, head into Marion where this route ends and the next begins. You'll find ten or more motels and a choice of restaurants and relaxation spots.

In the Area

All numbers are within area code 618.

Southern Illinois Tourism Council, P.O. Box 40, Whittington, IL 62897: 629-2506 or 800-342-3100

Carbondale Convention and Tourism Bureau: 800-526-1500

Williamson County Tourism Bureau (Marion): 800-433-7399

Murphysboro Chamber of Commerce: 684-6421

Shawnee Convention and Visitors Bureau (Ullin): 800-248-4373

Cairo Chamber of Commerce: 734-2737

John A. Logan Museum (Murphysboro): 684-3455

Shawnee National Forest Headquarters (Harrisburg): 253-7114

Oakwood Bottoms/Green Tree Reservoir: 687-1731

Ma Hale's Boarding House Restaurant (Grand Tower): 565-8384

La Rue-Pine Hills Ecological Area (Jonesboro): 833-8567

Union County Conservation Area: 833-5175

Horseshoe Lake Conservation Area (Miller City): 776-5689

Safford Memorial Library and Museum (Cairo): 734-1840

Magnolia Manor (Cairo): 734-0201

Wyndham Bed and Breakfast (Cairo): 734-3247

Limekiln Springs, Nature Conservancy (Ullin): 634-2231

Cache River State Natural Area (Little Black Slough/Heron Pond, Belknap): 634-9678

Paul Powell Home (Vienna): 658-4911

Trail of Tears State Forest (Jonesboro): 833-4910

Alto Vineyards (Cobden): 893-4898

Cobden Museum: 893-2067

Lawrence Box and Basket Factory (Cobden): 893-2354

Giant City State Park (Makanda): 457-4836

Giant City State Park Lodge (Makanda): 457-4921

Crab Orchard National Wildlife Refuge (Marion): 997-3344

13 ~

The

Southeast:

Hills and

History

From Chicago: Take I-57 south to Marion (about 300 miles).

From St. Louis: Take I-64 east to I-57 south to Marion (about 120 miles). The trip begins and ends in Marion.

Highlights: *Shawnee National Forest, wildlife and recreational areas, natural wonders and remote country towns; Native American and mid-1800s history; the "Deer Capital of Southern Illinois" and a World Championship Goose Calling Contest; Metropolis, the self-styled hometown of Superman.*

Shawnee National Forest's eastern regions are chock full of natural beauty—rock formations of sculpted sandstone, narrow canyons, caves, and long views over wooded hills and valleys. The national forest owes its existence to widespread unemployment in mining industries and failures of marginal farms during the Depression: in 1939, the government began purchasing much of the least productive land and turning it into a managed forest.

This is the empty quarter of Illinois, with the state's least populous counties. But it contains some of the most beautiful parks and preserves in the state. You'll zigzag through its scenic countryside to find wide vistas as well as outstanding sites for hiking, camping, horseback riding, birding, and botany. Along the way you'll also discover the remains of Native American settlements, a pirate's lair, the state's first financial hub, and a lonely mansion haunted with a macabre history of slave trade.

With a population of 14,000, the Williamson County seat of Marion is one of the main population centers of southern Illinois. New Route 13 whizzes through the north side of town, lined with fast-food restaurants and their strip-mall friends. Old Route 13 (Main Street) leads to the heart of town—Tower Square's tall red brick bell and clock tower.

In Marion, you can still find a one-man barber shop (with a vacuum cleaner hooked to the clippers), honest antique dealers, and restaurants with southern barbecue and southern hospitality. One busy night we chose to dine in the lounge rather than wait for a restaurant table at the long-time local favorite, Tony's Steak House and Lounge; the owners fussed over us like maiden aunts to be sure we weren't unhappy with our seats. Pulley's, a local hangout next to Mike's Country Fruit Market on old Route 13 east of downtown, serves a lip-smacking southern barbecue.

Marion's county fair, which begins each Labor Day, has run every year since pre-Civil War days. A younger event is National Hunting and Fishing Days at John A. Logan College (west of town), which includes the Winchester World Championship Goose Calling Contest.

Travel east from Marion to Harrisburg on Route 13, passing strip mines and land under reclamation. Turn south (right) on Route 45 to the headquarters of Shawnee National Forest for maps and information. Further along Route 45, Saline County Area Museum is housed in a former poor farm. It preserves the heritage of southern Illinois settlers in seventeen themed rooms of the old alms house. A typical 1890s parlor, dining room, bedroom, and kitchen portray home life; other rooms are devoted to printing, toys, photography, mining and minerals, medicine, law, and veterans. Early log buildings—a general store, a one-room school, an 1870 Quaker church, a blacksmith shop, and a log barn with one of the Midwest's last threshing floors—were moved to the grounds from surrounding hills.

Return to Route 13 and continue east along the flat valley of the Saline River. Mounds of strip mines rise to the south, backed by the edges of the Shawnee Hills in the distance. To the north, Southwestern Illinois College perches on hills between the river's branches.

Take a side trip to Old Shawneetown, hunkered beneath earthen levees along the Ohio River, which served as the earliest gateway for Illinois settlers and was the state's first financial hub. To get there, continue on Route 13 across Route 1, passing melon markets and coal mines. You first reach the new Shawneetown, which straggles along the highway. Its most eye-catching sight is a flashing neon pig advertising Rudy's barbecue, "Serving You Since '32." The majority of old Shawneetown's residents moved to this site above the Ohio River's bottomland after the worst recorded flood swelled five feet higher than the top of the levee in 1937.

Some 400 people still linger in Old Shawneetown, an agglomeration of trailers, empty shops, an abandoned school and church, a couple of taverns, a fish and bait shop, a few modest homes that survived the flood—and even fewer reminders of the town's heyday. It's hard to conceive that when Illinois joined the union in 1818, this was the state's financial center, welcoming a steady stream of settlers, goods, packets, and keelboats.

The handsome John Marshall House, a two-story brick structure with a matched pair of chimneys at each end, testifies to Shawneetown's thriving early days. In 1816, the house became the site of the first bank chartered in Illinois. Legend has it that in 1830, several men rode more than 300 miles from the settlement of Chicago to request a loan of $1,000 to improve their village. They were turned down; Chicago was too far from Shawneetown to amount to anything. Down the street, the shuttered First State Bank, a well-proportioned Greek Revival edifice built in 1839 as successor to the earlier bank, also bears witness to the town's long-gone wealth.

Return to the junction of routes 13 and 1, which is marked by a small motel and restaurant. Turn south (left) on Route 1 and follow signs pointing right up a lane to the Old Slave House, a southern colonial mansion that has been owned by George Sisk for the last thirty years. The mansion, called Hickory Hill, was built in 1834 by John Crenshaw on a lonely hilltop site overlooking the Saline River valley. Crenshaw had become wealthy and powerful by leasing and operating government-owned salt works at natural springs along the valley. Since labor was scarce, the government authorized the use of slaves in this corner of an otherwise free territory.

Crenshaw was also involved in the illegal trade of stolen slaves and captured runaways. He built into his mansion a driveway that ended inside the house, so that a carriage's human cargo could be unloaded secretly and hurried up to the third floor. There he used closet-size rooms flanking a narrow hallway as cells. Outside the low doorways you'll see whipping posts to which slaves were tied by their thumbs. Owner Sisk may retire and close the house, which would be unfortunate; this chilling insight into the brutal pre-Civil War slave trade should remain open to visitors.

Continue south on Route 1. A right turn on Pounds Hollow Road toward Karbers Ridge leads to a pair of recreation areas featuring rugged rock outcroppings. You arrive first at the Rim Rock/Pounds Hollow area, where the first access road leads to a beach on twenty-five-acre Pounds Hollow Lake. The man-made lake was created in a narrow wooded hollow typical of the Illinois Ozarks. From there, you can hike or drive to Rim Rock, a circular sandstone escarpment. In the last century, loggers used a huge overhang at the base of this rock as a shelter for oxen and horses. A paved trail leads uphill through hardwood trees, then circles the rim of the escarpment, which is covered by gnarled cedars.

Continue along the blacktop road through Karbers Ridge, a village with terrific views over the hills. You soon reach Garden of the Gods, where 200 million years of wind and water have transformed the sandstone bluffs into strange sculptures given names like Anvil Rock and Devil's Smokestack. Along with an easygoing observation trail, the park maintains a relatively undisturbed 3,300-acre wilderness area with primitive trails that draw serious hikers and horseback riders.

Backtrack to Route 1 and continue south through the wooded landscape into Cave-in-Rock, an Ohio River hamlet of 450 adjoining a small state park. A rock shop at the edge of town sells multicolored fluorspar, a mineral that was mined in Hardin County to make fluorine-containing chemicals. In town, you'll find a café, an ice cream shop, a floating fish market, and a ferry to Kentucky. Each June, the twenty-five-mile Davy Crockett Ohio River Relay Race of flatboats takes off from Cave-in-Rock and heads downstream for Golconda. The flatboats, made of lashed-together logs, are like those that brought settlers to Illinois. Canoes, kayaks, sailboats, and rowboats also join in the fun.

Cave-in-Rock State Park perches on a narrow strip of sixty-foot-high hills and rugged bluffs along the river. You can walk to a large cave that became the lair of river pirates who robbed and murdered unsuspecting travelers. In the park's cheerful restaurant, you can down a fried catfish sandwich while admiring long vistas across the river and the rolling Kentucky hills. Recently built cabins in the park are furnished with kitchenettes and private decks.

Backtrack on Route 1 to Route 146 and turn west (left), following the Ohio River. There's a turnoff to Tower Rock (there is another Tower Rock along the Mississippi across from Grand Tower), four miles down a gravel road, which is an off-the-beaten-path campsite and picnic area with more long views. Further along Route 146 is Hardin County's only school—kindergarten through twelfth grade.

The river community of Elizabethtown serves as Hardin County seat; the county has about 5,300 people and supports a single sheriff and part-time deputy. "There isn't much crime," said Don Phillips, who with his wife Elisabeth owns the River Rose Inn bed and breakfast overlooking the river. "Besides, we all know who the bad guys are." All five of the River Rose's rooms, decorated in antiques with a French influence, have river views. Across the street, the front porch of the Rose Hotel makes a visitor wish he'd brought along a rocking chair. Built in 1812, it is the oldest hotel in Illinois, though it now houses Jacqueline's River Gifts selling handmade baskets, quilts, dried flowers, dolls, jellies and jams, and other handicrafts.

With 1,400 people, Rosiclare is Hardin County's population center. This community, once supported by fluorspar mines, lies south of Route 146. A gravel road leads north from the Rosiclare intersection to a restored forty-two-foot-high iron furnace on Hog Thief Creek. Constructed in 1837 and enlarged just before the Civil War, this and other charcoal-fired furnaces sucked up trees from the surrounding forests for charcoal to smelt pig iron from local ore deposits. Until the furnaces closed in the 1880s, more than a hundred families made their living here. By 1938, the village's buildings were gone. Now the wooded site has picnic tables and (naturally) charcoal grills.

Return to Route 146, which leads into Pope County. With only 4,400 people, Pope is the state's most sparsely populated county—reflected in the modest courthouse and war memorial in Golconda. This county seat was where 10,000 Cherokees crossed the Ohio River into Illinois on their forced march west along the Trail of Tears during the winter of 1838–1839. A ferry operator charged them the exorbitant sum of $1.00 a head (the normal cost was 12^{1}/2¢ for a conestoga wagon and all you could carry) and forced them to wait until everyone else had crossed. At least one Golconda family, the Buells, reached out to the starving Indians by sharing their pumpkin crop.

Golconda bills itself as the "Deer Capital of Southern Illinois," hosting hunters after game in the forests to the north. Boaters and fishermen headquarter here, too; a state-operated marina rents boats. You'll also find casual restaurants, antique shops, and stables around town. Visitors seeking fine dining in an antique-filled room head for Mansion of Golconda, an inn owned by Don and Marilyn Kunz. A candlelight dinner might include sautéed chicken livers and spicy grilled catfish Camille served on antique platters, rounded out with fresh-baked bread and a homemade dessert like Almond Glory pie. Your room may have a canopy bed, a fireplace, a lace-draped mahogany headboard, or a whirlpool heated by an 1890s cast iron stove.

From Golconda, Route 146 turns west toward Dixon Springs State Park, just east of the Route 145 intersection. The 465-acre park surrounds seven mineral springs that became a nineteenth-century health spa. A small town with a general store, a post office, a blacksmith shop, a gristmill, and several churches grew up around the spa. The churches remain on a rocky hilltop overlooking the springs and a modern swimming pool with bathhouse and water slide. This lower level comprises a giant block of rock that dropped 200 feet along a fault line; deep in its moist and shady fissure, the rock is always cooler than the surrounding area. Trails lead past rugged cliffs, crags, and giant boulders fringed by ferns, ivy, lichens, and moss. A small creek shaded by century-old trees bubbles along a narrow canyon.

Across the highway from the park entrance, the Chocolate Factory may lure you in with the rich smell of creamy candies made on the spot, or with its wonderful ice cream selections.·

Take a super side trip. Proceed faster than a speeding bullet (but not over the legal limit) south on Route 145 from Dixon Springs to Metropolis, the self-styled hometown of Superman. The comic-book hero, clad in red and blue tights and cape, appears on welcoming billboards and the town's water tower. The chamber of commerce shows off photos and Superman gear, including a red and blue phone booth like the one the man from Krypton used as a changing room. A stumpy-legged statue of the airborne strongman stands on the courthouse square, to be replaced by a sleeker twelve-foot bronze model as soon as donations reach the required $100,000 level.

This homey little town sits on a flat stretch along the Ohio River. Overlooking the river at its east edge is a reconstructed replica of Fort Massac as it was built in 1794 by order of President George Washington. The site has a long history.

Some believe an original fort or trading post was founded here by the French as early as 1702. In 1757, several years after the start of the French and Indian War, soldiers from Fort de Chartres built a wooden stockade, though it was abandoned and burned by 1765.

In 1778, Colonel George Rogers Clark and his Virginia and Kentucky soldiers known as "The Long Knives" crossed the Ohio near the fort site. From there they marched 100 miles

Superman's "hometown" is Metropolis, Illinois

to Kaskaskia, which they captured from the British without a shot on the evening of July 4th. A statue of Clark looks out over the Ohio River traffic from the Massac site.

The palisade-style reconstruction, with two-story guardhouses at each corner, is the scene of almost-monthly living-history weekends and an annual fall encampment. It's a fine spot to camp, hike, and picnic.

After visiting Metropolis, go north on Route 145 toward Glendale. Tucked among the hills is the Dixon Springs Agricultural Center of the University of Illinois, a 4,930-acre outdoor laboratory that's the largest experimental station east of the Mississippi. Research is done in many fields, including forestry and wildlife. A self-guided driving tour takes visitors to an arboretum, along a trail of bluebird nest boxes, to an agroforestry patch in which crops are grown between rows of trees, and through areas that show how brush piles, food plots, and grown-up fence rows can be used to create wildlife habitat.

At Glendale, you have a choice of fascinating routes to Goreville, from which you'll return to Marion. The first is the fastest and easiest; it keeps to paved highways through the hills and stops at the remains of a prehistoric Indian settlement.

The alternative is for the more intrepid traveler. It takes a longer and more winding path, sometimes on slow-going gravel roads, via Bell Smith Springs, a remote national recreation area known for its scenery and variety of unusual plants.

If you choose the easier route, turn west (left) at Glendale on Route 147. In about a mile, you'll reach a sign pointing north (right) on a gravel road toward Millstone Bluff Archaeological Area. Stop here and take a hike. The half-mile walk along a well-maintained trail makes a steep, 320-foot ascent to a natural fortresslike area atop a wooded bluff where you'll come upon one of the few well-preserved prehistoric settlements in the Midwest. As you circle the site, illuminating signs point out the pits that were floors of twenty or so houses around a central plaza. This was a community of the Mississippian Indian culture 1,000 years ago.

The trail also reaches an exterior wall built 500 years earlier by Woodland Indians and passes stone-lined graves and rock-carved petroglyphs of spiders, an eagle with spread wings, peace pipes, and a circle enclosing a cross. Let your imagination wander while reading the sign: "As you look across the plaza, imagine a fall day, the air filled with smoke rising from cooking fires. Children play while their fathers repair a roof. Hunters return with their game as women grind corn and dry meat on tall racks in preparation for the long winter ahead."

Back on Route 147, you'll pass Trigg Observation Site, one of only a few fire watchtowers left. The forest is interrupted here and there by farms; most raise cattle, though some produce hogs and horses. Many have small man-made ponds to conserve soil and water. At Route 146 turn west (right) toward Vienna for a brief overlap with the previous route as far as West Vienna. Turn north (right) there on Route 37—you can't miss the pair of lawn ornament shops at the intersection.

The 1,100-acre Ferne Clyffe State Park lies just before Goreville. Its fifteen miles of trails—from easy to difficult—lead through gorges and canyons, past impressive rock formations to wide vistas. Early this century, Emma Rebman, Johnson County school superintendent, bought this scenic spot and in 1929 began charging admission to the grounds. In 1949, the state bought the original 140 acres from her, added to it, and built a sixteen-acre lake. Campsites and equestrian trails now round out the facilities.

One of Ferne Clyffe's most unusual rock formations is a 150-foot-long shelter bluff called Hawks' Cave, reached by the easy quarter-mile Rebman Trail. More than 700 kinds of plants grow in the park, which was named for its abundance of ferns. A wildflower show bursts forth in late April and early May, and fall colors take over in October.

If you choose the alternate route to Goreville, at Glendale head northeast on Route 145 to the town of Eddyville. From there, a sign toward Bell Smith Springs Recreation Area points you west and north through the forests to the park's turnoff. The springs feed Bay Creek, which flows through a ravine etched out of sandstone bluffs. Sugar maple, tulip, and beech trees grow below, surrounded by upland hickory and oak. More than 700 kinds of ferns and flowering plants have been identified at Bell Springs. These include some survivors of the last Ice Age, like leatherwood and the threatened hay-scented fern, sheltered along cool, shaded creek bottoms. This is the only spot in Illinois where they are found.

Hikers who descend into Bay Creek canyon can choose a trail to a natural bridge that is thirty feet high, twenty feet wide, and more than 125 feet long. Another path passes spring-fed pools that make great swimming holes, before leading to the remains of an old gristmill.

When you leave the park turn west (left) and follow signs toward US 45. After a gravel stretch that seems to last forever, the road becomes paved again as you cross into Johnson County. In Ozark, a square barber pole is wired to a tree outside a home.

When you reach US 45, turn south (left) for several miles to Tunnel Hill Road, where signs for Tunnel Hill and Lake of Egypt take you west (right) again. The road swoops over wooded hills and past cattle farms through an area full of lakes. Shortly after crossing I-24 you'll reach Route 37 near Ferne Clyffe State Park.

North of Goreville, you can stop in the fall to pick some apples at Eastman Orchards; their roadside stand also sells cider, peaches, and other seasonal produce. Further up the road, eavesdrop on a rapid-fire cattle auction at Goreville Livestock, which shares a rambling building with the Longhorn Restaurant, open from 6:00 A.M. to 2:00 P.M. (or whenever the auction ends). One would expect the steaks to be fresh.

From Goreville, Route 37 rolls past forests, farms, and small towns, out of Shawnee National Forest and back into Marion, where we began.

In the Area

All numbers are within area code 618.

Southern Illinois Tourism Council, P.O. Box 40, Whittington, IL 62897: 629-2506 or 800-342-3100

Williamson County Tourism Breau (Marion): 800-433-7399

Shawnee Convention and Visitors Bureau (Ullin): 800-248-4373

Metropolis Chamber of Commerce: 524-2714

Shawnee National Forest Headquarters (Harrisburg): 253-7114

Tony's Steak House and Lounge (Marion): 993-2220

Saline County Area Museum (Harrisburg): 253-7342 or 253-5085

Old Shawneetown Historical Society: 269-3303

Old Slave House (Hickory Hill, Equality): 276-4410

Rim Rock/Pounds Hollow Recreation Area (Elizabethtown): 287-2201

Garden of the Gods Recreation Area (Elizabethtown): 287-2201

Cave-in-Rock State Park: 289-4325

Cave-in-Rock Lodge and Restaurant: 289-4545

River Rose Inn (Elizabethtown): 287-8811

Illinois Iron Furnace (Rosiclare): 287-2201

Golconda Marina: 683-5875

Mansion of Golconda Restaurant and Bed and Breakfast: 683-4400

Dixon Springs State Park (Golconda): 949-3394

Fort Massac State Park (Metropolis): 524-4712

Dixon Springs Agricultural Center: 695-3383

Ferne Clyffe State Park (Goreville): 995-2411

Bell Smith Springs Recreation Area (Vienna): 658-2111

Index

Index

Index

Index

Index

Peterstown House, Waterloo, 127, 137

Pierre Menard Home, Ellis Grove, 131–132, 137

Postville Courthouse Historic Site, Lincoln, 90, 99

Randolph County Courthouse, Chester, 134

Rasmussen Blacksmith Shop, Lewistown, 67, 71

Reddick Mansion, Ottawa, 45, 48

Reorganized Church of Jesus Christ of Latter Day Saints Visitors Center, Nauvoo, 76, 83

Ronald Reagan Boyhood Home, Dixon, 25, 26

Ryan barn, Kewanee, 51–52

Safford Memorial Library & Museum, Cairo, 145, 151

Saline County Area Museum, Harrisburg, 154–155, 165

St. Mary's covered bridge, Bremen, 136

Stephenson County Historical Society Museum, Freeport, 14

Stronghold, The, Oregon, 20, 26

Time Museum, Rockford, 16

Tinker Swiss Cottage, Rockford, 16

Western Museum, Macomb, 82, 83

Will County Historical Society I & M Canal Museum, Lockport, 40–41, 48

Wyatt Earp home, Monmouth, 57

National Hunting & Fishing Days, Marion, 154

National Shrine of Our Lady of the Snows, Belleville, 134, 138

Native American statue, Oregon, 20–21

nature centers, see parks

Nauvoo, 72–77, 82–83

Nauvoo State Park, 76, 83

Nauvoo Mill & Bakery, 77

Nauvoo Glassworks, 77

New Boston, 59

New Boston Museum, 59

New Salem, 86–89, 99

New Salem Historical Site, 87–88

Nick's Tavern, Lemont, 40, 48

1905 Emporium, antiques, Richmond, 29

"Norma Jean" elephant grave, Oquawka, 58

Northern Illinois University Lorado Taft Field Campus, Oregon, 22

Oak Hill Cemetery, Lewistown, 67–68

Oak Ridge Cemetery, Lincoln Tomb, Springfield, 93, 99

Oakland Cemetery, Petersburg, 89

Oaks, The, Bed & Breakfast and Smoot Hotel, Petersburg, 95, 99

Oakville Country School Museum, Mount Carroll, 13

Oakwood Bottoms Green Tree Reservoir, 141, 151

Och's Christmas Tree Farm, Galena, 10, 14

Octoberfest, Carthage, 81

Oglesby, Richard J., 97

Old Church House Inn, Mossville, 71

Old Kaskaskia Trading Post, 133

Old Shawneetown, 155–156, 165

Old Slave House (Hickory Hill), Equality, 156, 165

Old State Capitol, Springfield, 92, 98

Olde English Faire, Jubilee College, Brimfield, 70

Oogies Drive-in, Ottawa, 45

Oquawka, 57–58

Orchard Hill Farm, Lewistown, 66, 71

Oregon Public Library, 22

Oregon, 20–24, 25

Ottawa, 45

otters, 53

parks, wildlife areas, zoos, and gardens
  Alice L. Kibbe Life Science Station, Warsaw, 78, 83
  Apple River Canyon State Park, 5, 14
  Argyle Lake State Park, Colchester, 81–82, 83
  Bald Knob Mountain, 148–149
  Banner Marsh State Fish and Wildlife Area, Canton, 63, 70
  Bell Smith Springs Recreation Area, Vienna, 164, 166
  Big River State Forest, Keithsburg, 58, 60
  Blanding Landing Recreation Area, 11–12
  Buffalo Rock State Park, Ottawa, 45, 48

175

Index

Index

Acknowledgments

I want to thank my husband, Jack, who acted as chauffeur and fellow observer on our journeys along the routes of this book. Special thanks, too, to Ann Ridge of the Illinois Bureau of Tourism for her encouragement and knowledgeable assistance.

I'd like to extend my heartfelt appreciation to the dozens of people at local and regional tourism bureaus and chambers of commerce, who not only provided enormous amounts of information, but did so with an infectious enthusiasm and love for their towns and byways.

These people also deserve thanks for providing background information that proved of great help: Joan and Marlowe Werkheiser of Freeport; Marilyn Daleo of Chicago; Arlene and Woody Robinson of Macomb; Dale Hoppe, Lorado Taft Field Campus, Northern Illinois University; Mary Ann Pitchford, Green Tree Inn, Elsah; David Braswell, Corner George Inn, Maeystown; Jean Gray, *The Nature of Illinois* magazine; Norma A. Turock, Nancy Moore, and Don Teel of the Cooperative Extension Service; and Jerry Clampet, Illinois Agricultural Statistics Service.

——*Marcia Schnedler*